# I AM *a* SON *of* SAINT AUGUSTINE

# I AM *a* SON *of* SAINT AUGUSTINE

## POPE LEO XIV *on* HIS FAVORITE SAINT

*Edited by* MATTHEW BECKLO

*Foreword by* SISTER MARGARET ATKINS, OSA

WORD *on* FIRE

Published by Word on Fire, Elk Grove Village, IL 60007

Printed in the United States of America


Cover design, typesetting, and interior art direction by Rozann Lee, Clark Kenyon, and Nicolas Fredrickson



ISBN: 978-1-68578-319-8

Library of Congress Control Number: 2025945367

# *Contents*

*I am an Augustinian, a son of Saint Augustine, who once said, "With you I am a Christian, and for you I am a bishop." In this sense, all of us can journey together toward the homeland that God has prepared for us.*

—Pope Leo XIV
First Blessing *Urbi et Orbi*
May 8, 2025

# *Foreword*

Sister Margaret Atkins, OSA

*Unless stated otherwise, all quotations of Pope Leo XIV in the foreword are from this collection.*

"I am a son of Saint Augustine," Pope Leo declared in his first *Urbi et Orbi* blessing. But what did he mean? We know he is an Augustinian friar. What, though, is the deeper significance of that?

Let me begin with a story. I was speaking recently with Father Ian Wilson, OSA, a friend of our community. Father Ian is also an Augustinian friar and lives with his brothers at the Augustinian Curia in Rome, where Father Robert Prevost, OSA, was based as prior general, and where Cardinal Prevost was still sharing their community life until the day the conclave began. "I'm really missing Bob," said Father Ian. He then described how Bob Prevost would be there in chapel first thing every day, meditating quietly before joining the friars for Morning Prayer and Mass. After a morning's work just across the road in the Vatican, he would return for lunch, slipping in a few minutes late because of the timetable. If the pasta was cold, he quietly got up and warmed it up in the microwave. He was always enjoyable and humorous company. No fuss, no show, just another member of the community. Shared prayer, shared conversation, a shared life.

Augustinian ideals are not just theory; they are lived experience. They are all there in Father Ian's anecdote: unity, love, and peace; friendship and community; service and Church; truth, prayer, and the search for God. They were lived out together each day by Friar Bob and his brothers, as they were many centuries earlier by Saint Augustine (354–430) and his. This "human experience is actually the door that leads one into discovering who God is." Let's look a bit more closely at these elements and how they interrelate.

The pope's motto is *In Illo uno unum*, "In that One, [we are] one." (The words come from a homily by Augustine on Psalm 128.) "That One," of course, is Christ. Augustinian brothers and sisters follow a "Rule" that Augustine himself originally wrote for his own communities. It is a kind of handbook for life together. Right at the beginning it says, "The main purpose for you having come together is to live harmoniously in your house, intent upon God in oneness of mind and heart." For Saint Augustine, this was something joyful. He took delight in the opening of Psalm 133: "How very good and pleasant it is when kindred live together in unity!"

Augustinian living is organized around the idea of building unity, which Augustine sees as equivalent to peace and to love. No wonder Pope Leo's first public words were "Peace be with you all," while in his inaugural homily he proclaimed, "This is the hour for love!"

It is our unity that enables us to seek God. The best-known line Saint Augustine wrote was "Fecisti nos ad Te et inquietum est cor nostrum donec resquiescat in Te," which literally means, "You made us toward Yourself and our heart is restless until it rests in You." Translators often write, "Our hearts *are* restless," but for Augustine, our restless search for God has to be a shared one, lived out with our *one* heart. "Every dimension of the common life which strengthens unity among the brothers is an aid in fostering the search for God."

Our unity, then, is not inward-looking, focused on ourselves. We are to be of one mind and heart *in Deum*—that is, "on the way to God." This outward-looking approach spills over to other human beings. The love of God, as Augustine loved to quote, "has been poured into our hearts through the Holy Spirit" (Rom. 5:5), and it is expressed in love of strangers as well as friends. It flows especially, of course, toward those in need. Again, this was not just theory but reality for Augustine, whose role as a bishop included both organizing relief for the poor and encouraging his flock to support this. Similarly, Pope Leo learned how to be a pastor among poor parishioners, and also refugees, in Peru. Thus, through the lived experience of overflowing love, communities centered on God expand and interweave to form a worldwide network of unity. In the pope's twelve years as prior general, he visited communities of brothers on every continent and encountered the daily work they did immersed in their local communities. That assignment, along with his gift for languages, has especially equipped him to understand this love as both personal and global.

In the same homily in which Saint Augustine says, "In that One, one," he describes Christians as the children of Christ, and asks, "What kind of people are they?" His answer is "Peacemakers." And he goes on to explain that there is no peace without charity. Augustine, whose own church was called the "Basilica of Peace," was here thinking primarily of divisions within the Church. But his profound meditation on peace, love, and unity, flowing from our hearts to our neighbors to the world, has wider implications. Pope Leo, called to care for human souls under the shadow of "wars and rumors of wars" (Matt. 24:6), deeply understands the connection between peace in our hearts, in our churches, and among nations.

Communities of any size are only as good as those in charge. It is significant that the young Father Prevost chose to write his thesis on the office and authority of the local prior. He emphasizes there how the prior must be totally focused on fostering the unity of his brothers in their common search for God. "There is no room in Augustine's concept of authority for one who is self-seeking and in search of power over others." Authority must be a selfless service of love, for enabling others to love. That is why office in the Church is not a privilege to be sought but rather, as Augustine often said, a burden to be accepted in charity. Leaders must never forget that first and foremost they are fellow Christians, brothers or sisters of those in their care.

Because this Augustinian unity—this love and fellowship—is real lived experience, it naturally develops into friendship. Saint Augustine wrote, "I find it easy to give myself entirely to the love of those who are my intimate friends. . . . In this love I am perfectly at ease, because in it I experience God" (*Letter* 73.10). As Cardinal Prevost put it, "The gift of friendship brings us back to Jesus himself." It is not surprising that Augustinian communities overflow into an extended Augustinian family—for example, the lay fraternities mentioned in this collection. The welcome in such communities ought to be warm (and in my experience always is). As the *Constitutions* of my own Augustinian Federation beautifully puts it, our hearts "are transformed by the Holy Spirit into places where someone who is a stranger becomes a brother or sister."

For Augustine, though, love was never just about warm feelings. Our shared search for God is a shared search for *truth*, for Christ who is the Truth. That is why education matters. Pope Leo, grateful for his own time at school and university, spoke of the Augustinians' "very significant contribution to the role of the Church in education."

That is why listening matters. Leo has outlined a "theology of listening," linking it both with the role of priors and with the current movement of "synodality," which he calls "this great ongoing process." We listen to each other, in the Holy Spirit, in order to learn. We also listen to those outside the Church, such as the pagan poet Terence, quoted by Saint Augustine: "Nothing that is truly human is foreign to me."

Above all, that is why it matters to listen to God's Word. "The Word of God alone enables the person to recognize the truth" and "calls us together as a community." Pope Leo reminds us that the first thing Saint Augustine did when called to be a priest was beg the bishop to allow him a few months off to study Scripture. His request was granted.

The passages of Scripture that spoke most to Augustine about community were Acts 2:41–47 and Acts 4:31–35, which both describe the shared life of the early Christians. Pope Leo emphasizes that they listened to the Holy Spirit before they "spoke the word of God." They also "broke bread" together. This phrase included shared meals, which give both physical life and friendship. Its focus, though, was the bread of the Eucharist, which builds the Body of Christ into one, "the creative force of real Christian community."

The Augustinian community modeled on Acts is a living cell of the Church, there to serve the wider Body of Christ. That is why Father Prevost's thesis described the role of the prior as "ecclesial," of and for the Church. This community is also a small-scale version of what the whole Church should be: united in heart and mind *in Deum*. Conversely, it is Christ, our Truth, who brings our deepest unity. We are one Body in him as Head: The "whole Christ," as Augustine loved to say, is Christ with his Church. It is fitting that in Pope Leo's first address to the cardinals, he named as the first of his evangelical principles "the return to the primacy of Christ in proclamation."

Another of Leo's brother friars, Father Noel Hession, OSA, preached on the day after the election of his "joy, excitement, and hope, because I know this man, and I believe that in choosing him the assembled cardinals in the conclave have given a great gift to the Church." Pope Leo XIV is perhaps an especially valuable gift to the Church at this moment. Pope Francis led us toward a more "synodal" way of being Church. Many of the faithful are still struggling to comprehend what this means. Pope Leo's experience of Augustinian community life, combined with his clarity of Augustinian vision and his global experience, can help us, as a worldwide Church, to understand it and bring it to life. He knows how patient, loving attentiveness to the Spirit working through one another can guide us to grow toward the truth, in unity of mind and heart, in our shared search for God. "Brothers and sisters," he urged us at his installation, "I would like that our first great desire be for a united Church, a sign of unity and communion, which becomes a leaven for a reconciled world."

I hope you all enjoy exploring these themes, in Pope Leo's own words and in those of Saint Augustine, his mentor and inspiration. Let us pray that this little book may help us to be of one heart and one mind on the way to God, in the Church led by Pope Leo XIV, a living sign of the unity for which Christ prayed.

# *Timeline*

**September 14, 1955:** Robert Francis Prevost is born at Mercy Hospital in Chicago, Illinois.

**1969–1973:** Attends Saint Augustine Seminary High School near Saugatuck, Michigan, earning a letter of commendation for academic excellence.

**1977:** Earns a bachelor of science degree in mathematics from Villanova University, a university founded by the Order of Saint Augustine in 1842 near Philadelphia, Pennsylvania.

**September 1, 1977:** Joins the Order of Saint Augustine as a novice.

**September 2, 1978:** Takes his first vows in the Order.

**August 29, 1981:** Takes his solemn vows in the Order.

**June 19, 1982:** Is ordained a priest at the church of Saint Monica of the Augustinians in Rome.

**1982:** Earns a master of divinity degree from Catholic Theological Union in Chicago, teaching at Saint Rita of Cascia High School, operated by the Order of Saint Augustine, during his studies.

**1984:** Earns a licentiate in canon law at the Pontifical University of Saint Thomas Aquinas in Rome.

**1985:** Joins the Augustinian mission in Peru, serving as chancellor of the Territorial Prelature of Chulucanas.

**1987:** Earns a doctorate in canon law at the Pontifical University of Saint Thomas Aquinas; his doctoral thesis is titled *The Office and Authority of the Local Prior in the Order of Saint Augustine*.

**1987:** Goes on to serve as vocation director and missions director of the Augustinian province of Our Mother of Good Counsel in Olympia Fields, Illinois, and work with the faculty of the Augustinian novitiate in Oconomowoc, Wisconsin.

**1988–1998:** Returns to Peru, serving as head of the Augustinian seminary in Trujillo, teaching canon law, and working in parish ministry; in Trujillo, he also serves as local prior—the subject of his doctoral thesis—from 1988 to 1992.

**1998:** Is elected prior provincial of the Order of Saint Augustine's Province of Our Mother of Good Counsel, assuming the role on March 8.

**2001–2013:** Serves two six-year terms as prior general of the Order of Saint Augustine; during these twelve years, he lives in Rome but travels around the world, including to Augustinian provinces in Nigeria and the Philippines.

**2013–2014:** Serves as director of formation at the Convent of Saint Augustine in Chicago and as first councilor and provincial vicar of the Province of Our Mother of Good Counsel.

**May 16, 2014:** Receives honorary doctor of humanities degree from Villanova.

**November 3, 2014:** Is appointed apostolic administrator of the diocese of Chiclayo.

**December 12, 2014:** Is consecrated a bishop at Saint Mary's Cathedral in Chiclayo, taking the motto *In Illo uno unum* (In that One, [we are] one) from Saint Augustine.

**2015–2023:** Serves the people of Chiclayo as bishop.

**September 30, 2023:** Is made a cardinal by Pope Francis.

**2023–2025:** Serves as prefect of the Dicastery for Bishops and president of the Pontifical Commission for Latin America.

**May 8, 2025:** Is elected as the 267th bishop of Rome, taking the name Leo XIV; his coat of arms includes his Augustinian episcopal motto and a red heart aflame and pierced by an arrow—the emblem of the Order of Saint Augustine, symbolizing the heart burning with love for God.

# *Coat of Arms*

I

# On Saint Augustine's Life and Works

## ***Beginning with Biography***

In order to approach a figure of such great personality as Augustine of Hippo, it is not only a legitimate methodological option, but also, in the case of Augustine, a necessity to start from his biography. The wealth of his human experience in and of itself, along with the effect of that same experience upon his writings, makes it clear that such a methodological approach serves as an important guide to understanding his thought. It is no coincidence that one of his major works is autobiographical, the *Confessions*. And not without reason can it be affirmed that behind so many of Augustine's ideas the attentive reader can find the deeply human and passionately lived experience from Augustine's own life. Without a doubt, this is where the continued relevance of Augustine's thought and his powerful attraction are rooted: "I am human, one of many, I live among humans and I have a human heart. . . . Nothing that is truly human is foreign to me" [a quotation of the Roman poet Terence—see *Sermon* 323.2; *Letter* 78.8; *On the Trinity* 4.1; *Letter* 155]. Those who begin to know Augustine discover that he speaks to his readers with the same passion as if he were speaking today.

—Foreword to *Saint Augustine*, 2007

## *The Grace and Peace of God*

As Augustinians, we strive every day to live up to the example of our spiritual father. . . . So much of who I am I owe to the spirit and the teachings of Saint Augustine. . . .

Saint Augustine, as you know, was one of the great founders of monasticism; a bishop, theologian, preacher, writer, and Doctor of the Church. But this did not happen overnight. His life was full of much trial and error, like our own lives. But through God's grace, through the prayers of his mother, Monica, and the community of good people around him, Augustine was able to find the way to peace for his restless heart.

The life of Saint Augustine and his call to servant leadership reminds us that we all have God-given gifts and talents, and our purpose, fulfillment, and joy comes from offering them back in loving service to God and to our neighbor. . . .

Like Augustine, we come together with our moments of anxiety, darkness, and doubt, and just like Augustine, through God's grace, we can discover that God's love is truly healing.

—Message to the Augustinian Province
of Saint Thomas of Villanova, August 29, 2025

## *A Summary of Augustine's Ministry*

After receiving baptism, [Augustine decided] to begin a life that we can call monastic, religious. He decided to put aside his ambitions, his career, and his desire to have a family. He already had a son, Adeodatus, but upon receiving baptism, he decided to dedicate his life to God, to the search for God: to live with that great restlessness—so typical, so important in Augustine's life—seeking God, and seeking to love, seeking friendship, seeking to live in community, this great search.

Then, having been baptized in Milan, he decided to return to his homeland, passing through Rome. While at the port of Ostia, waiting for his passage to return with his mother and his son, Saint Monica died there in Ostia Antica. From Ostia, Augustine returned to Tagaste, the place where he was born. There, he established a monastery with a group of friends to live out that search. However, sometime later, he went to visit a city not far from Tagaste, a city called Hippo (today Annaba, in the north of Algeria). Augustine was well known, and the bishop of Annaba, of Hippo, whose name was Valerius, recognized Augustine and called him, saying, "I need a priest here to assist me." Valerius was Greek and did not speak Latin very well, and he needed someone to assist him in his ministry, so he called Augustine.

Augustine, who was present, had no intention, no desire, to enter the priestly ministry. But one Sunday, he experienced a calling. He began to weep because he knew that when the Lord calls, you must answer him. And then some people commented, "Look! He is crying because he is being called to be a priest, not to be a bishop." But Augustine said, "Nothing could be further from the truth." He was crying—he felt this pain—because he was going to have to leave his community, his monastery, to go to another place and serve as a priest. And he accepted the call very generously. He said, "Lord, you have called me. Here I am."

But he asked one thing of Valerius. He said, "I have to

study the Word of God" [see *Letter* 21]. Another element in this continuous conversion of Augustine that marks his life and can also be an example for us is how important it is to study and reflect on the Word of God because it is the Word of God that calls us together as a community, and where we find the message of love, salvation, life, and freedom. So, Augustine dedicated himself to study for a few months, and then, for four years, he assisted Valerius as a priest.

When Valerius passed away, Augustine was called and became bishop of Hippo, and served for over thirty years as bishop of Hippo. In his episcopal ministry, there are elements that we find earlier in Augustine's life. As a bishop, he has to listen to many people. He is, in a sense, the judge. He has to help people seek justice. He is always very concerned about the well-being of the poor; charity is very important. He has beautiful and important writings and sermons telling people, "Look, the things you have are not yours. You have received them from God. But if you have much, and someone else does not, it is not your right to withhold what does not belong to you." And so he encourages everyone to be in solidarity, to seek ways to share what they have received, to help the most vulnerable, the neediest—a lesson that is very important for all of us today.

There are other themes in Augustine's life as a bishop: a great deal of time, many sermons, participation in many councils, or councils of bishops, because Augustine dedicated much of his energy and time to the idea of unity. In the same city of Hippo, there was the cathedral of Augustine, called the Basilica of Peace, but there was another cathedral belonging to a sect or a community that had separated from the Catholic Church—a group called the Donatists. Augustine was deeply grieved by this division in the Christian community because Jesus Christ is one, and his Body is one, and when there is division, there is pain, and we do wrong. Augustine always insisted on this and greatly emphasized the need to seek unity among all believers, all the faithful—a stance that would also be very good for us. . . .

As a bishop, Augustine was also deeply dedicated to that first quest, which was also a driving force throughout his life: seeking the truth. More and more, we see the great value and necessity of the truth in society, in the world we live in, especially with "fake news," with so many lies circulating on social media, with the ease with which people can criticize one thing, make up another, say that this is the way it is when it is not so. Always seek the truth. God is truth, and he calls us as a community to be seekers of this same truth. We are sons and daughters of Augustine, and we also have to recognize that truth is an essential element in our lives, as is the quality of love, friendship, community, and communion.

Although as a bishop, he was called out of his monastery, Augustine decided to live with a group of priests, of clerics, because that style of life—of living in community, sharing life, sharing faith—was a very fundamental element in the life of Augustine and also in his episcopal ministry.

—Message to Our Lady of the Rosary Parish
in Chitré, Panama, 2020

## *Preferential Love for the Poor*

The holy Bishop of Hippo taught for his part about the preferential love for the poor. A vigilant pastor and theologian of rare insight, he realizes that true ecclesial communion is expressed also in the communion of goods. In his commentaries on the Psalms, he reminds us that true Christians do not neglect love for those most in need: "Observing your brothers and sisters, you know if they are in need, but if Christ dwells in you, also be charitable to strangers" (*Expositions of the Psalms* 125.12). This sharing of goods therefore stems from theological charity and has as its ultimate goal the love of Christ. For Augustine, the poor are not just people to be helped, but the sacramental presence of the Lord.

The Doctor of Grace saw caring for the poor as concrete proof of the sincerity of faith. Anyone who says they love God and has no compassion for the needy is lying (see 1 John 4:20). . . .

In a Church that recognizes in the poor the face of Christ and in material goods the instrument of charity, Augustine's thought remains a sure light. Today, fidelity to Augustine's teachings requires not only the study of his works, but also a readiness to live radically his call to conversion, which necessarily includes the service of charity.

—*Dilexi Te*, apostolic exhortation, October 4, 2025

## *Monk-Bishops*

Saint Augustine . . . speaks of the *Life of Antony* in the *Confessions* (8.14.15). But in the West, the ascetic movement took on a different direction, and there are many examples of men who, while being devoted to the monastic life, lived in a manner that was very much given to the carrying out of pastoral duties. Augustine and Martin of Tours are just two examples of "monk-bishops," and there are many other examples of men who were recruited from monasteries to become priests or bishops. One of the results that came about . . . was that the style of religious, charismatic authority was institutionalized.

—Doctoral dissertation, 1987

## *Opening a Window*

God is not someone or something that is absent and far away, and Augustine—in his spirituality, in his struggles, in his reflections that we see for example in the *Confessions*—is able to open a window, if you will, and to lead others to come to discover how God is working in their lives.

—Interview with Rome Reports, 2013

## *The "Confessions" and Human Experience*

One of the reasons that the *Confessions* continues to be one of the widest-read books in the history of the world is precisely because of Augustine's insight into human experience. And he does a magnificent job of communicating both his own experience and what he lived, and how that experience can indeed be a window, if you will, an opening to discovering a personal experience of God in human life. Human experience, he says, is precisely where you *can* find God, and the humanity of Augustine is not something which leads into a kind of personalized, egoistic, "it's all about me and only me" world, but quite the opposite because of Augustine's understanding of humanity: that human experience is actually the door that leads one into discovering who God is.

And then a movement that Augustine speaks of in different areas [is] how going into God also leads you into solidarity with other people. That second part of living in solidarity with others is perhaps a piece of the experience that is missing nowadays. So often today in the highly individualistic society that people are growing up in, people think that "my experience" is *the* criterion: "Am I happy or not happy?" What that might really be is: "Do I feel pleasure or don't I feel pleasure?" Or, "Do I feel selfish, and if I feel okay then that's all that matters." And I think that certainly Augustine's experience says that that isn't enough, and maybe what you're calling happiness isn't authentic happiness, because you're going to lose that too. Most things that people seem to describe as "Well, why are you happy today?" are things that are either very superficial or at best important for a short period of time but aren't going to last forever. And Augustine gives some insight into helping people understand that having an experience of God brings you far beyond yourself, and includes that dimension of what I would call human solidarity, of understanding the universal brotherhood, sisterhood, of men and women; and that an authentic experience of happiness has to include other people and has to include being concerned about other people. Those are elements that express, I think, a very important part of the Gospel message. It's not just about me and my experience of God either. You might have people say, "Oh, I have an experience of God, and I don't have to do anything else." Well, then that's probably not an authentic experience of God, because as we know from the Gospels, as we know from the apostolic letters, if you love God then you also need to be showing that by loving your neighbor, and the two go hand in hand.

So experience can be a wonderful tool, if you will, to help bring people into an experience of Christ in their lives, of God in their lives. Augustine in the *Confessions* talks about friendship, talks about family, talks about the importance of his mother, talks about his father, talks about human ambition, talks about so many different aspects of human life, and then goes on to explain how these things helped or did not help his own personal pathway to discovering God and to discovering what is really holy about life.

—Interview with Catholic News Service, 2012

## *"The City of God" Today*

To find our footing in the present circumstances—especially you as Catholic legislators and political leaders—I suggest that we might look to the past, to that towering figure of Saint Augustine of Hippo. As a leading voice of the Church in the late Roman era, he witnessed immense upheavals and social disintegration. In response, he penned *The City of God*, a work that offers a vision of hope, a vision of meaning that can still speak to us today.

This Church Father taught that within human history, two "cities" are intertwined: the City of Man and the City of God. These signify spiritual realities—two orientations of the human heart and, therefore, of human civilization. The City of Man, built on pride and love of oneself, is marked by the pursuit of power, prestige, and pleasure; the City of God, built on love of God unto selflessness, is characterized by justice, charity, and humility. In these terms, Augustine encouraged Christians to infuse the earthly society with the values of God's kingdom, thereby directing history toward its ultimate fulfillment in God, while also allowing for authentic human flourishing in this life. This theological vision can anchor us in the face of today's changing currents: the emergence of new centers of gravity, the shifting of old alliances, and the unprecedented influence of global corporations and technologies, not to mention numerous violent conflicts. The crucial question before us believers, therefore, is this: How can we accomplish this task? . . . In your vocation as Catholic lawmakers and public servants, you are called to be bridge-builders between the City of God and the City of Man.

—Address to Catholic legislators, August 23, 2025

## *A Response to the Secular World*

The Church Fathers offered a formidable response to those non-Christian and anti-Christian literary and rhetorical forces at work throughout the Roman Empire in shaping the religious and ethical imaginations of the day. The *Confessions* of Saint Augustine, with its central image of the *cor inquietum* [restless heart], has shaped the way that Western Christians and non-Christians reimagine the adventure of religious conversion. In his *City of God*, Augustine used the tale of Alexander the Great's encounter with a captured pirate to ironize the supposed moral legitimacy of the Roman Empire. . . . They understood with enormous precision the techniques through which popular religious and ethical imaginations of their day were manipulated by the centers of secular power in that world.

—Address to the World Synod of Bishops on the New Evangelization, 2012

## *The Myths of Secular Society*

The Fathers of the Church have a great deal to contribute because of a number of parallel or similar circumstances that the Church lived in the first centuries, that the Church is living today. . . . [Think of] Saint Augustine and the encounter between the emperor and the pirate, and . . . the kinds of myths that society can promote, the kind of attitudes that can fool people into thinking that this is what you're really looking for when in reality it can be very superficial or even an outright lie.

—Interview with Catholic News Service, 2012

## *"De Magistro" and the Inner Master*

By imitating Sister Maria Teresa, [the foundress of the Augustinian Sisters, Servants of Jesus and Mary,] you will therefore be patient in tribulations, because it is precisely in our trials that the Lord confirms his faithfulness; you will be courageous in the mission, so that the educational work to which you dedicate yourselves may form wise minds and hearts capable of listening and of passion for humanity; you will be unwavering in the following of Christ, who is "the way, the truth, and the life" (John 14:6), and therefore the criterion for all our cultural initiatives. We know that a culture without truth becomes an instrument of the powerful: Instead of freeing consciences, it confuses and distracts them according to the interests of the market, fashion, or worldly success.

In this regard, I advise you to pick up again a work by the holy Doctor, our father Augustine, *De Magistro*, to contemplate it in the near future, as you gather the fruits of your Chapter. In this work, Augustine affirms that external teaching must always lead to the encounter with the inner Master, who is Jesus (see 1.11).

—Greeting to the Augustinian Sisters, Servants of Jesus and Mary, July 5, 2025

## *The First Modern Man*

Monk, bishop, and doctor of the Church, Augustine of Hippo obviously transcends the limits of Church history and religious doctrine. Frequently given the title of the first modern man, Augustine is the protagonist of one of the most moving autobiographies ever written, as well as having been one of the most influential thinkers in Western culture, and an author who perhaps has analyzed the phenomena of religious experience in greater depth than anyone. Without a doubt, all of these aspects contribute to the fact that Augustine continues to be of such relevance today, and to his continuing ability to draw the attention of women and men, believers or otherwise, intellectuals or simple searchers, of the twenty-first century.

—Foreword to *Saint Augustine*, 2007

2

# *On Saint Augustine's Spirituality*

## ***Made Restless by History***

I greet all of you with a heart full of gratitude at the beginning of the ministry that has been entrusted to me. Saint Augustine wrote: "Lord, you have made us for yourself, and our heart is restless until it rests in you" (*Confessions* 1.1). . . .

With the light and the strength of the Holy Spirit, let us build a Church founded on God's love, a sign of unity, a missionary Church that opens its arms to the world, proclaims the word, allows itself to be made "restless" by history, and becomes a leaven of harmony for humanity.

—Homily for papal inauguration Mass, May 18, 2025

## ***Begin with Your Own Heart***

We have to look beyond our own—if you will—egotistical ways. We have to look for ways of coming together and promoting a message of hope. Saint Augustine says to us that if we want the world to be a better place, we have to begin with ourselves, we have to begin with our own lives, our own hearts (see *Sermon* 311; *Tractates on the Gospel of John* 77). . . .

We all live with many questions in our hearts. Saint Augustine speaks so often of our "restless" hearts and says: "Our hearts are restless until they rest in you, O God" (*Confessions* 1.1). That restlessness is not a bad thing, and we shouldn't look for ways to put out the fire, to eliminate or even numb ourselves to the tensions that we feel, the difficulties that we experience. We should rather get in touch with our own hearts and recognize that God can work in our lives, through our lives, and through us reach out to other people.

—Video message to the young people of Chicago
and the whole world, June 14, 2025

## *Return to the Heart*

Just as Jesus loved with a human heart, so you are called to love with the Heart of Christ! To learn this art, however, you need to work on your interior life. . . . Keep in mind Saint Augustine's constant invitation to return to the heart, because it is there that we will find God. Sometimes descending to the depths of our heart can be intimidating, since we also have to confront our hurts, our wounds. Yet do not be afraid to face them, also with the help of others, because those wounds will make you sympathetic and compassionate towards others who suffer. Without an interior life, no real spiritual life is possible, because it is in the heart that God speaks to us.

—Meditation for the Jubilee of Seminarians, June 24, 2025

## *God Is Closer to Us than We Are to Ourselves*

The whole concept of the new evangelization needs to begin with a personal encounter with Jesus Christ. People have to in some way be led or invited into an experience where they can rediscover what it means to have faith, what it means to have a relationship with Jesus Christ, what it means to recognize that God is indeed a part of our lives. Saint Augustine would say that God is closer to us than we are to ourselves [see *Confessions* 3.6]. But the reality in society today is that people have become alienated from the God who does dwell within us. And so to help people rediscover the presence of God, to rediscover the meaning of a relationship with Jesus Christ, is a big challenge, but I think that's what the starting point is.

—Interview with Catholic News Service, 2012

## *The Secret of Hope*

This is a rule of faith and the secret of hope: All this earth's goods, material realities, worldly pleasures, economic prosperity, however important, cannot bring happiness to our hearts. Wealth often disappoints and can lead to tragic situations of poverty—above all the poverty born of the failure to recognize our need for God and of the attempt to live without him. A saying of Saint Augustine comes to mind: "Let all your hope be in God: Feel your need for him, and let him fill that need. Without him, whatever you possess will only make you all the more empty" (*Expositions of the Psalms* 85.3).

—Message for the Ninth World Day of the Poor, June 13, 2025

## *I Burned for Your Peace*

We continually aspire to something "more" that no created reality can give us; we feel a deep and burning thirst that no drink in this world can satisfy. Knowing this, let us not deceive our hearts by trying to satisfy them with cheap imitations! Let us rather listen to them! . . .

Saint Augustine, reflecting on his intense search for God, asked himself: "What, then, is the object of our hope? . . . Is it the earth? No. Is it something that comes from the earth, such as gold, silver, trees, crops, or water? . . . These things are pleasing, these things are beautiful, these things are good" (*Sermon* 313/F.3). And the conclusion he reached was: "Seek the one who made them, he is your hope" (ibid.). Thinking of his own journey, he prayed, saying: "You [Lord] were within me, but I was outside, and it was there that I searched for you. . . . You called, you shouted, and you broke through my deafness. You flashed, you shone and you dispelled my blindness. You breathed your fragrance on me; I drew in breath and now I pant for you. I have tasted you (see Ps. 34:8; 1 Pet. 2:3) now I hunger and thirst for more (see Matt. 5:6; 1 Cor. 4:11); you touched me, and I burned for your peace" (*Confessions* 10.27). . . .

Sisters and brothers, these are beautiful words. . . . There is a burning question in our hearts, a need for truth that we cannot ignore, which leads us to ask ourselves: What is true happiness? What is the true meaning of life? What can free us from being trapped in meaninglessness, boredom, and mediocrity?

—Homily for Mass for the Jubilee of Youth, August 3, 2025

## *God Is Your Everything*

Saint Augustine, speaking of the primacy of God in the Christian life, affirms that "God is your everything. If you are hungry, God is your bread; if you are thirsty, God is your water; if you are in darkness, God is your light that never fades; if you are naked, God is your everlasting garment" (*Tractates on the Gospel of John* 13.5). Indeed, we would do well to ask ourselves: To what extent are these words true for me? How much does the Lord satisfy my thirst for life, love, or light?

—Address to women's religious institutes, June 30, 2025

## *Lord, Your Works Praise You*

With infinite love, God has created all things and given them life. That is why Saint Francis of Assisi could call every creature his brother, his sister, and his mother. Only a contemplative gaze can change our relationship with creation and bring us out of the ecological crisis brought on by the breakdown of our relationship with God, with our neighbors, and with the earth that is the effect of sin (see *Laudato Si'* 66). . . .

I would like to conclude these thoughts by leaving you with the words with which Saint Augustine, in the last pages of his *Confessions*, brought together creation and humanity in a cosmic hymn of praise: Lord, "your works praise you, that we may love you; may we love you, that your works may praise you" (13.33). May this be the harmony that we spread throughout the world.

—Homily for Mass for the Care of Creation, July 9, 2025

## *Do Not Delay!*

In the light of [the parable of the laborers in the vineyard in Matthew 20], today's Christian might be tempted to think, "Why start work immediately? If the pay is the same, why work more?" Saint Augustine responds to these doubts, saying: "Why then do you put off him that calls you, certain as you are of the reward, but uncertain of the day? Take heed then lest perhaps what he is to give you by promise, you take from yourself by delay" (*Sermon* 37.8).

I would like to say, especially to the young, do not wait, but respond enthusiastically to the Lord who calls us to work in his vineyard. Do not delay, roll up your sleeves, because the Lord is generous and you will not be disappointed! Working in his vineyard, you will find an answer to that profound question you carry within you: What is the meaning of my life?

—General audience, June 4, 2025

## *Living Up to Our Calling*

The character who accompanies us in this reflection will help us to understand that we must never give up hope, even when we feel lost. He is Bartimaeus, a blind man and a beggar, whom Jesus meets in Jericho (see Mark 10:46–52). . . .

Bartimaeus means "son of Timaeus": The man is described through a relationship, and yet he is dramatically alone. This name, though, could also mean "son of honor" or "of admiration," exactly the opposite of the situation in which he finds himself. (This is the interpretation also given by Augustine in *The Harmony of the Gospels* 2.65.125; PL 34:1138.) And since the name is so important in Jewish culture, it means that Bartimaeus fails to live up to what he is called to be. . . .

What saves Bartimaeus, and each one of us, is faith. Jesus heals us so that we can become free. He does not invite Bartimaeus to follow him, but tells him to go, to set out on his way (see Mark 10:52). However, Mark concludes the story by saying that Bartimaeus began to follow Jesus: He freely chose to follow him, he who is the Way!

—General audience, June 11, 2025

## *The Man Who Was Needed*

Jesus asks the paralytic a question that may seem superfluous: "Do you want to be well?" (John 5:6). Instead, it is a necessary question, because when one is stuck for so many years, even the will to heal may fade. Sometimes we prefer to remain in the condition of sickness, forcing others to take care of us. It is sometimes also an excuse for not deciding what to do with our lives. Jesus instead takes this man back to his truest and deepest desire.

Indeed, this man replies in a more articulate way to Jesus's question, revealing his true vision of life. He says first of all that he has no one to immerse him in the pool: So he is not to blame, but the others who do not take care of him. This attitude becomes the pretext for avoiding responsibility. But is it really true that he had no one to help him? Here is Saint Augustine's enlightening answer: "Truly he had need of a 'man' to his healing, but that 'man' who is also God. . . . He came, then, the Man who was needed: Why should the healing be delayed?" (*Tractates on the Gospel of John* 17.7).

—General audience, June 18, 2025

## *Faith Touches*

Around Jesus there is a large crowd, and therefore many people were touching him, and yet nothing happens to them. Instead, when [the bleeding woman] touches Jesus, she is healed. Where does the difference lie? In his commentary on this point of the text, Saint Augustine says—in Jesus's name—"The crowd jostles, faith touches" (*Sermon* 243.2.2). It is thus: Every time we perform an act of faith addressed to Jesus, contact is established with him, and immediately his grace comes out from him. At times we are unaware of it, but in a secret and real way, grace reaches us and gradually transforms our life from within.

—General audience, June 25, 2025

## *Grant What You Command, Command What You Will*

It was precisely at particular moments of trial that Christ revealed the Father's will: It was when challenged by the Pharisees that he taught us that the two greatest commandments are to love God and our neighbor (see Matt. 22:34–40). It was on the eve of his Passion that he spoke of the need for unity, "that all may be one . . . so that the world may believe" (John 17:21). My wish for each of us, then, is that we can say with Saint Augustine: "My entire hope is exclusively in your very great mercy. Grant what you command, and command what you will" (*Confessions* 10.29).

—Message to participants in the Commemoration of 500 Years of the Anabaptist Movement, May 29, 2025

## *The Holy Spirit Descends Upon Us*

"The day has dawned upon us when . . . , glorified by his Ascension into heaven following his Resurrection, the Lord Jesus Christ sent the Holy Spirit" (Saint Augustine, *Sermon* 271.1). Today, too, what took place in the Upper Room takes place anew in our midst. Like a mighty wind that overtakes us, like a crash that startles us, like a fire that illuminates us, the gift of the Holy Spirit descends upon us (see Acts 2:1–11).

—Homily for the Solemnity of Pentecost, June 8, 2025

## *Both Listening and Service*

Saint Augustine, reflecting on the story of Martha and Mary in one of his homilies, said: "These two women symbolize two lives: the present and the future; a life lived in toil and a life of rest; one troubled and the other blessed; one temporary, the other eternal" (*Sermon* 104.4). And considering Martha's work, Augustine said: "Who is exempt from the duty of caring for others? Who can rest from these tasks? Let us try to carry them out with charity and in such a way that none will be able to find fault with us. . . . The weariness will pass and rest will come, but rest will only come through the effort made. The ship will sail and reach its homeland; but the homeland will not be reached except by means of the ship" (ibid., 6–7).

Today, . . . Martha and Mary remind us that listening and service are two complementary attitudes that enable us to open ourselves and our lives to the blessings of the Lord. Their example invites us to reconcile contemplation and action, rest and hard work, silence and the bustle of our daily lives with wisdom and balance, always taking Jesus's charity as our measure, his Word as our light, and his grace as our source of strength, which sustains us beyond our own capacity (see Phil. 4:13).

—Homily for Mass at the Cathedral of Albano, July 20, 2025

## *Let Us Forgive*

Although all of us are called to be ministers of Christ, the physician of souls, for our brothers and sisters (see Luke 5:31–32), we are ourselves frail and in need of healing. As Saint Augustine said, using the image of a ship, all of us "have in this life some cracks in our frail mortality, through which sin trickles in from the waves of this world" (*Sermon* 278.13). And the holy bishop of Hippo proposes a remedy for evil: "Lest we sink," he says, "let us hold fast to this exhortation. . . . Let us forgive" (ibid.).

—Address to the Servants of the Paraclete, June 6, 2025

## *Becoming the Good Samaritan*

Pope Francis, who often reminded us that God is mercy and compassion, once referred to Jesus as "the compassion of the Father toward us" (Angelus, July 14, 2019). Saint Augustine tells us that, as the Good Samaritan who came to our aid, Jesus "wanted to be known as our neighbor. Indeed, the Lord Jesus Christ makes us realize that he is the one who cared for the half-dead man beaten by robbers and left on the side of the road" (*De Doctrina Christiana* 1.30.33).

We can understand, then, why this parable is so challenging for each of us. If Christ shows us the face of a compassionate God, then to believe in him and to be his disciples means allowing ourselves to be changed and to take on his same feelings. It means learning to have a heart that is moved, eyes that see and do not look away, hands that help others and soothe their wounds, shoulders that bear the burden of those in need.

—Homily for Mass at the Pontifical Parish
of Saint Thomas of Villanova, July 13, 2025

## *Transformation in Love*

The works of mercy are the most secure and profitable bank where we can entrust the treasure of our existence, because there, as the Gospel teaches us, with "two small copper coins" even the poor widow becomes the richest person in the world (Mark 12:41–44).

In this regard, Saint Augustine says: "If you gave a pound of coppers and received a pound of silver, or a pound of silver and received one of gold, you would be delighted at your luck. What you give will certainly be transformed; it isn't gold, it isn't silver, but eternal life that will come your way" (*Sermon* 390.2). And he explains why: "It will be transformed, because you yourself will be transformed" (ibid.). . . . Therefore, wherever we are, in the family, parish, school, or workplace, we should try not to miss any opportunity to act with love.

—Angelus address, August 10, 2025

## *Following Christ Means Joining the Church*

When I think of Saint Augustine, his vision and understanding of what it means to belong to the Church, one of the first things that springs to mind is what he says about how you cannot say you are a follower of Christ without being part of the Church. Christ is part of the Church. He is the Head.

So people who think they can follow Christ "in their own way" without being part of the Body, are, unfortunately, living a distortion of what is really an authentic experience. Saint Augustine's teachings touch every part of life, and help us to live in communion.

Unity and communion are essential charisms of the life of the Order and a fundamental part of understanding what the Church is and what it means to be in it.

—Interview with Ricardo Morales Jiménez, 2023

## *No One Is Christian Alone*

The desire to work together for a common purpose reflects an essential reality: No one is Christian alone! We are part of a people, a Body established by the Lord. When speaking of Jesus's first disciples, Saint Augustine once said, "They became God's temple, not only as individuals; together they were built into the temple of God" (*Expositions of the Psalms* 131.5). The Christian life is not lived in isolation, as a kind of intellectual or sentimental experience, confined to the mind and the heart. It is lived with others, in a group and in community, because the risen Christ is present wherever disciples gather in his name.

—Address to the Moderators of Lay Associations,
Ecclesial Movements, and New Communities,
June 6, 2025

## *Bread That Restores and Does Not Run Short*

Our hungry nature bears the mark of a need that is satisfied by the grace of the Eucharist. As Saint Augustine writes, Christ is truly "panis qui reficit, et non deficit; panis qui sumi potest, consumi non potest" (*Sermon* 130.2): He is bread that restores and does not run short; bread that can be eaten but not exhausted. The Eucharist, in fact, is the true, real, and substantial presence of the Savior (see *Catechism of the Catholic Church* 1413), who transforms bread into himself in order to transform us into himself. Living and life-giving, the *Corpus Domini* makes us, the Church herself, the Body of the Lord.

—Homily for the Solemnity of Corpus Christi, June 22, 2025

## *The Sacrifice and Gift of Love*

Let us think of how wonderful it is when we give a gift—even a small one, proportionate to our means—and see that it is appreciated by the recipient; how happy we are when the gift, despite its simplicity, unites us even more to those we love. Indeed, what happens between us and God through the Eucharist is precisely that the Lord welcomes, sanctifies, and blesses the bread and wine that we place on the altar, together with the offering of our lives, and he transforms them into the Body and Blood of Christ, the sacrifice of love for the salvation of the world. God unites himself to us by joyfully accepting what we bring, and he invites us to unite ourselves to him by likewise joyfully receiving and sharing his gift of love. In this way, says Saint Augustine, "Just as one loaf is made from single grains collected together . . . so in the same way the body of Christ is made one by the harmony of charity" (*Sermon* 229/A.2).

—Angelus address for Corpus Christi, June 22, 2025

## *Harmony in Diversity*

Dear friends, the history of Peter and Paul shows us that the communion to which the Lord calls us is a unison of voices and personalities that does not eliminate anyone's freedom. Our patron saints followed different paths, had different ideas, and at times argued with one another with evangelical frankness. Yet this did not prevent them from living the *concordia apostolorum*, that is, a living communion in the Spirit, a fruitful harmony in diversity. As Saint Augustine remarks, "The feast of the two Apostles is celebrated on one day. They too were one. For although they were martyred on different days, they were one" (*Sermon* 295.7.7).

—Homily for the Solemnity of Saints Peter and Paul, June 29, 2025

## *A Family of God*

This Church [is a] communion of believers, enlivened by the Holy Spirit, who enables us to enter into the perfect communion and harmony of the blessed Trinity. Indeed, it is in the Trinity that all things find their unity. This dimension of our Christian life and mission is close to my heart, and is reflected in the words of Saint Augustine that I chose for my episcopal service and now for my papal ministry: *In Illo uno unum*. Christ is our Savior and in him we are one, a family of God, beyond the rich variety of our languages, cultures, and experiences.

—Address to the Pontifical Mission Societies, May 22, 2025

## *A Sign of Unity*

[Peter] is called to serve the faith of his brothers and sisters, and to walk alongside them, for all of us are "living stones" (1 Pet. 2:5), called through our baptism to build God's house in fraternal communion, in the harmony of the Spirit, in the coexistence of diversity. In the words of Saint Augustine: "The Church consists of all those who are in harmony with their brothers and sisters and who love their neighbor" (*Sermon* 359.9).

Brothers and sisters, I would like that our first great desire be for a united Church, a sign of unity and communion, which becomes a leaven for a reconciled world.

In this our time, we still see too much discord, too many wounds caused by hatred, violence, prejudice, the fear of difference, and an economic paradigm that exploits the Earth's resources and marginalizes the poorest. For our part, we want to be a small leaven of unity, communion, and fraternity within the world. We want to say to the world, with humility and joy: Look to Christ! Come closer to him! Welcome his word that enlightens and consoles! Listen to his offer of love and become his one family: *In the one Christ, we are one*. This is the path to follow together, among ourselves but also with our sister Christian churches, with those who follow other religious paths, with those who are searching for God, with all women and men of good will, in order to build a new world where peace reigns!

—Homily for papal inauguration Mass, May 18, 2025

## *We Will All Be One*

The prayer of the Son of God, which gives us hope on our journey, also reminds us that one day we will all be *uno unum* (see Saint Augustine, *Expositions of the Psalms* 127.3): one in the one Savior, embraced by the eternal love of God. Not only us, but also our fathers, mothers, grandmothers, grandfathers, brothers, sisters, and children who have already gone before us into the light of his eternal Pasch.

—Homily for Mass for the Jubilee of Families, June 1, 2025

## *The Communion of Christians*

Saint Augustine, in a homily delivered on the anniversary of his ordination, spoke of the joyful fruit of communion that unites the faithful, priests, and bishops, grounded in the recognition that all of us are redeemed and saved by the same gracious mercy of God. It was in that context that he spoke the celebrated words: "For you I am a bishop, with you I am a Christian" (*Sermon* 340.1).

—Homily for Mass for the Jubilee of Priests, June 27, 2025

## *Listening as Much as Possible*

The Diocese of Rome has undertaken [a challenging process of listening] in these years, a process carried out at various levels. . . .

For my part, I would like to express my firm desire to contribute to this great ongoing process by listening to everyone as much as possible, in order to learn, understand, and decide things together, as Saint Augustine would say, "as a Christian with you and a bishop for you" (see *Sermon* 340.1).

—Homily for Mass for the possession of the chair of the bishop of Rome, May 25, 2025

## *The Mindset of Synodality*

Go forward in unity, thinking especially of the synodal path. The Lord, Saint Augustine writes, "in order to keep his body well-composed and in peace, exhorts the Church, through the Apostle Paul: 'The eye cannot say to the hand, I do not need you, nor again the head to the feet, I do not need you. If the whole body were an eye, where would the hearing be? If the whole body were hearing, where would the sense of smell be?'" (*Expositions of the Psalms* 130.6). Stay united and do not defend yourselves against the provocations of the Spirit. Synodality becomes a mindset, in the heart, in decision-making processes and in ways of acting.

—Address to the Italian Episcopal Conference, June 17, 2025

## *The "Amoris Officium"*

The whole life of the bishop, his entire ministry, diverse and multifaceted as it is, finds its unity in what Saint Augustine calls the *amoris officium* [duty of love]. Here his theological life is expressed and shines forth in the highest degree. Whether preaching, visiting communities, listening to priests and deacons, or making administrative decisions, all that he does is inspired and motivated by the charity of Christ the Shepherd. With the help of God's grace, drawn daily from the celebration of the Eucharist and his prayer, the bishop gives an example of fraternal love to his coadjutor or auxiliary, to the bishop emeritus and to the bishops of neighboring dioceses, to the priests, his closest collaborators, particularly those experiencing moments of difficulty or illness. His heart is open and welcoming, and so is his home.

—Meditation for the Jubilee of Bishops, June 25, 2025

## *One Flock and One Shepherd*

Let us entrust our priestly life to the Lord, and let us ask him to be able to grow in unity, in exemplarity, and in prophetic commitment to serve our time. May we be accompanied by the heartfelt appeal of Saint Augustine, who said: "Love this Church, continue to be in such a Church, be such a Church yourselves; love the good shepherd, so beautiful a husband, who deceives no one, desires no one to perish. Pray also for the scattered sheep; may they come in too, may they too recognize, they too love this Church, so that there may be one flock and one shepherd" (*Sermon* 138.10).

—Address to the clergy of Rome, June 12, 2025

# 3

# *On Saint Augustine's Thought*

## ***Eschatology, Anthropology, and Christian Hope***

The thought of Saint Augustine is of continued relevance in the life of the Church. The German theologian Adolf Harnack called Augustine "the first modern man." More recently, Pope John Paul II clearly stated that Saint Augustine continues to be present in today's culture, as he has much to say to the world today, through what he writes and in the example he gives. Saint Augustine is always relevant to the times, because he is concerned about the most pressing problems of human life, and among those we find, of course, one of the ultimate questions of humanity: What is our destiny? Where are we going? A question that is inseparable from two other interrogatives that constitute the central issue in the anthropological question: Where did we come from and who are we? Eschatology, in effect, is for Augustine a basic element not only in theology, but also in anthropology. "Life within this mortal existence is the basis for hope in immortality" (*Expositions of the Psalms* 103, sermon 4.17). The human being is in constant search of happiness, and this desire for true happiness is an essential part of that permanent human desire to find life and immortality. "There is no greater life than an eternal and happy life, given that if it is not eternal, it is not happy" (*Sermon* 306.6). . . .

Saint Augustine understands life as a long process that is enlivened and energized precisely because of hope. "While the traveler, after all, finds it wearisome walking along, he puts up with the fatigue precisely because he hopes to arrive. Rob him of any hope of arriving, and straightaway, his strength is broken for walking" (*Sermon* 158.8). This is undoubtedly an affirmation that Augustine based on his own experience, and which, from the viewpoint of faith, reaches even greater importance. Christians share with all humans the virtue of hope in this life, but they have greater hope in the promise of eternal life, guaranteed by the Resurrection of Christ and strengthened by the promise that only God can offer: "What God has promised you, he will give you; he does not deceive you, because he who has promised is Truth. Are you afraid he may not have it to give? He is almighty. Do not fear, either, that he may no longer be there to give it, for he is immortal" (*Expositions of the Psalms* 35.13). . . .

For Saint Augustine, bodily resurrection is a constitutive element of Christian eschatology. All too often, there has been a unilateral and equivocal affirmation of the Platonic and Manichean influences that persisted in the development of Saint Augustine's writings, and not only in his early writings. Augustine is accused of being negative and judgmental in his understanding of the human body and in all that is related to the material dimension. Yet, it is clear to those who know Saint Augustine that in his anthropology, body and soul form one integral reality that has been created and redeemed by God: "The human consists of body and soul, and when God redeems us, he does so in our integrity. The

Savior assumed our humanity in its integrity, so deigning to redeem in us the totality that he created" (*On Continence* 26).

This integral understanding of humanity acquires greater relevance in Augustine's theology, which will give great emphasis to the reality of Christ's humanity, insisting upon the intimate connection between the Incarnation and the Resurrection. We see this clearly in Augustine's interpretation of chapter 15 of Saint Paul's First Letter to the Corinthians, in which Saint Paul speaks of the resurrection of the body as a constitutive element in Christian eschatology. . . . Belief in the resurrection of the body is an essential and distinctive characteristic of Christianity, in relation to the Resurrection of Christ as well as in the question of the resurrection of all believers. This conclusion becomes evident through an understanding of Saint Augustine's theory of "Totus Christus," the "Total Christ," the Body's Head and its members. The Head is already risen and is the reason and the guarantee for the resurrection of all the members of the one Body. . . .

Our secularized and materialistic world, especially in the West, needs to be reminded of this important message that brings hope. And Saint Augustine makes it clear: Believers today need to be reminded of the bodily resurrection and of eternal life, to be strengthened in the faith that we share. We do not need to look for some kind of refuge in theories of reincarnation or cloning in order to find the true meaning of human life. Our faith in the resurrection of the body nourishes the hope that we have of finding true happiness which transcends the limits of our present condition. In spite of our limitations and of the problems of this world, we find ourselves enlightened by our belief in the Resurrection of Jesus Christ, the root of our dignity and our hope, he who is the Liberator of our human condition in all its dimensions.

—Foreword to *Augustine on the Hope of Groaning Creation*, 2006

## *Why Do You Stand in Your Own Strength?*

[I would] like to recall a passage from the conversion of Saint Augustine, as he himself relates it to us in his *Confessions*. On the one hand he was eager to decide for Christ; on the other, he was held back by scruples and temptations. Profoundly troubled, one day he retreated to reflect in the garden at home; and the personification of the virtue of Continence appeared to him, saying: "Why do you stand in your own strength, and so standest not? Cast yourself upon Him; fear not, He will not withdraw that you should fall; cast yourself upon Him without fear, He will receive you, and heal you" (*Confessions* 8.27).

As a father, I repeat these same words to you, which were so good for Augustine's restless heart: They do not apply only with regard to celibacy, which is a charism to be acknowledged, conserved, and educated, but can guide your entire journey of discernment and formation in ordained ministry. In particular, these words invite you to have boundless trust in the Lord, the Lord who called you, renouncing the pretense of being sufficient for yourselves or of being able to do it alone. And this applies not only to the seminary years, but to your whole life: At all times, all the more so in those of desolation or even sin, repeat to yourselves the words of the psalmist: "I trust in God's mercy forever and ever" (Ps. 52:10).

—Address to seminarians of the dioceses of Triveneto, June 25, 2025

## *Chosen Before Choosing*

Saint Paul [says] that he received from God the *grace* of his vocation (see Rom. 1:5). He acknowledges, in other words, that his encounter with Christ and his own ministry were the fruit of God's prior love, which called him to a new life while he was still far from the Gospel and persecuting the Church. Saint Augustine, who was also a convert, spoke of the same experience in these words: "How can we choose, unless we have first been chosen? We cannot love, unless someone has loved us first" (*Sermon* 34.2). At the root of every vocation, God is present, in his mercy and his goodness, as generous as that of a mother (see Isa. 66:11–13) who nourishes her child with her own body for as long as the child is unable to feed itself (see *Expositions of the Psalms* 130.9).

—Homily for the visit to the tomb of Saint Paul, May 20, 2025

## *Thirst for the Infinite*

The profound thirst for the infinite present in the heart of every human being means that parents have the duty to make their children aware of the fatherhood of God. In the words of Saint Augustine: "As we have the source of life in you, O Lord, in your light we shall see light" (*Confessions* 13.16 [see Ps. 36:9]).

Ours is a time marked by a growing search for

spirituality, particularly evident in young people, who are longing for authentic relationships and guides in life. Hence, it is important that the Christian community be farsighted in discerning the challenges of today's world and in nurturing the desire for faith present in the heart of every man and woman. . . .

Faith is primarily a response to God's love, and the greatest mistake we can make as Christians is, in the words of Saint Augustine, "to claim that Christ's grace consists in his example and not in the gift of his person" (*An Unfinished Work against Julian* 2.146). How often, even in the not too distant past, have we forgotten this truth and presented Christian life mostly as a set of rules to be kept, replacing the marvelous experience of encountering Jesus—God who gives himself to us—with a moralistic, burdensome, and unappealing religion that, in some ways, is impossible to live in concrete daily life.

—Message to participants in the seminar
"Evangelizing with the Families of Today and Tomorrow:
Ecclesiological and Pastoral Challenges," May 28, 2025

## *The Trinity and Divine Wisdom*

In [the book of Proverbs] we heard these words: "Thus says the wisdom of God: The Lord possessed me, the beginning of his ways, the forerunner of his prodigies of long ago. . . . When the Lord established the heavens I was there . . . then was I beside him as his craftsman, and I was his delight day by day, playing before him all the while, playing on the surface of his earth; and I found delight in the human race" (Prov. 8:22, 27, 30–31). For Saint Augustine, the Trinity and wisdom are intimately connected. Divine wisdom is revealed in the Most Holy Trinity, and wisdom always leads us to truth.

—Homily for the Solemnity of the Holy Trinity, June 15, 2025

## *Devouring the Word*

I think Pope Benedict finds in so many different parts of Augustine elements of his spirituality, of his love of the word of God, of the need to—as the prophets say, as Augustine says—devour the word of God and to delve into the beauty that God reveals to us through his word. Augustine did that constantly, and I think Pope Benedict does that in his own writing, in his own preaching, time and again. And he finds in Augustine, I think, kind of an echo of some of his own experience—as a man, as a pastor, as bishop, and as theologian.

—Interview for *The Papacy of Reason*, 2008

## *Seeds Sown in the Universe*

Be generous in sharing what you learn and what you experience, as best you can and however you can. Do not hesitate to share the joy and the amazement born of your contemplation of the "seeds" that, in the words of Saint Augustine, God has sown in the harmony of the universe (see *On the Literal Interpretation of Genesis* 5.23, 44–45). The more joy you share, the more joy you create, and in this way, through your pursuit of knowledge, each of you can contribute to building a more peaceful and just world.

—Address to participants of the summer school of astrophysics, June 16, 2025

## *Building the City of God*

*Religious freedom and interreligious dialogue* . . . [have] taken on greater significance in the present time, and political life can achieve much by encouraging the conditions for there to be authentic religious freedom and that a respectful and constructive encounter between different religious communities may develop. Belief in God, with the positive values that derive from it, is an immense source of goodness and truth for the lives of individuals and communities. Saint Augustine spoke of the need to pass from *amor sui*—egotistic, myopic, and destructive self-love—to *amor Dei*—a free and generous love, grounded in God and leading to the gift of self. That passage, he taught, is essential for the building of the *civitas Dei*, a society whose fundamental law is charity (see *City of God* 14.28).

—Address to Inter-Parliamentary Union, June 21, 2025

## *We Are the Times*

We are living in times that are both difficult to navigate and to recount. They present a challenge for all of us, but it is one that we should not run away from. On the contrary, they demand that each one of us, in our different roles and services, never give in to mediocrity. The Church must face the challenges posed by the times. In the same way, communication and journalism do not exist outside of time and history. Saint Augustine reminds of this when he said, "Let us live well and the times will be good. We are the times" (*Sermon* 80.8).

—Address to representatives of the media, May 12, 2025

## *Augustine's Theory of Education*

[Augustine] elaborates his theory of education in *De Magistro*, in a form of a discussion between himself and his son, Adeodatus. A teacher does not cause the student to think or to recognize the truth. A teacher can only stimulate the student to use his own talents, by use of illustrations and arguments. If the student is to see the truth for what it is, he needs an internal Teacher who shows truth directly to the minds of his students: The Word of God alone enables the person to recognize the truth.

—Doctoral dissertation, 1987

## *Let Us Sing*

The Roman polyphonic tradition, besides leaving us an immense heritage of art and spirituality, continues even today, in the sphere of music, to be a point of reference to look to, albeit with due adaptations, in sacred and liturgical composition, so that through song, "all the faithful should be led to that fully conscious and active participation in liturgical celebrations" (*Sacrosanctum Concilium* 14), with the profound involvement of voice, mind, and heart. . . .

Saint Augustine, speaking of the chant of the Easter Alleluia, said: "So now, my dear brothers and sisters, let us sing. . . . In the way travelers are in the habit of singing; sing, but keep on walking. . . . Make some progress, make progress in goodness. . . . Sing, and keep on walking. Don't stray off the road, don't go back, don't stay where you are" (*Sermon* 256.3). Let us embrace his invitation, especially in this holy time of the Jubilee.

—Address on the five-hundredth anniversary of the birth of Palestrina, June 18, 2025

## *Augustine on Friendship*

Saint Augustine tells us there is no friendship that is authentic if it is not in Christ. And the true friendship is always in Jesus Christ with truth, love, and respect. Only in him can it be eternal and happy (see *Against Two Letters of the Pelagians* 1.1.1). The one who loves God in his friend, truly loves his friend (see *Sermon* 336), Saint Augustine tells us. Friendship with Christ, which forms the basis of faith, is not just one aid among many others for building the future; it is our guiding star.

—Dialogue with young people, August 2, 2025

## *Augustine on Old Age*

In the Bible, God repeatedly demonstrates his providential care by turning to people in their later years. This was the case not only with Abraham, Sarah, Zechariah, and Elizabeth, but also with Moses, who was called to set his people free when he was already eighty years old (see Exod. 7:7). God thus teaches us that, in his eyes, old age is a time of blessing and grace, and that the elderly are, for him, the first witnesses of hope. Augustine asks, "What do we mean by old age?" He tells us that God himself answers the question: "Let your strength fail, so that my strength may abide within you, and you can say with the Apostle, 'When I am weak, then I am strong'" (*Expositions of the Psalms* 70.11). The increasing number of elderly people is a sign of the times that we are called to discern, in order to interpret properly this moment of history.

—Message for the Fifth World Day for Grandparents and the Elderly, July 27, 2025

## *Augustine on Mourning*

Early this morning I received the sad news of a companion of yours traveling with you on pilgrimage, your fellow pilgrim, your sister who passed away unexpectedly last night. . . . Saint Augustine tells us that when someone dies of course it is very human and very natural to cry, to feel that pain, to feel the loss of someone who is dear to us, and yet he also says, do not mourn as pagans do, because we too have seen Jesus Christ die on the cross and rise from the dead. . . . Our hope is in Jesus Christ who is risen. And he calls all of us to renew our faith, calls all of us to be friends, brothers and sisters to one another, to support one another, and he says you too must be witnesses to that Gospel message.

—Address to young Egyptian pilgrims, August 2, 2025

## *A Great Debt*

I have personally a great debt to the Order of Saint Augustine, to Saint Augustine himself, [his] philosophy, theology, thought, humanity; that great love of Augustine for God's word, that infinite searching for truth, for himself, and for God in himself; and for everything that

Augustine taught in terms of communion and community that marked my life.

—Reflection with Saint Jude Catholic Church
in New Lenox, Illinois, 2024

# 4

# *On the Order of Saint Augustine*

## *Two Great Sources*

The Order has as a founder, not an individual, but two great sources out of which the foundation was established: Saint Augustine and the Church. In a visit by Pope John Paul II to the Augustinians on May 7, 1982, his address in the chapel of the International College emphasized the very special circumstances which combined to create the Order as it exists today, and which give the Order those characteristics which provide its specific Augustinian identity:

> Having been called to govern the Church in this period of history, I cannot forget the special origin of your Order. Indeed, it was born in the very heart of the middle ages through the initiative of my predecessors Innocent IV and Alexander IV, and for this reason it is different from other religious institutes, taking a characteristic shape amid the vast range of the different canonical forms and structures for the profession of the evangelical counsels. Your Order, while relating to the letter and the spirit of the Augustinian *Rule* and bearing the lofty and noble title which Augustine's very name gives it, has holy Mother Church for the foundress of its juridic reality.

> Augustine and the Church, then. Two great names, my dear brothers, which combine to define your specific characteristics as religious. The heritage of the former and the very reality of the latter (of which, needless to say, Augustine is an unsurpassed teacher because of the depth of his ecclesial insights) urge you to live in a very close and exemplary communion of life, to practice and express this life in ways that are always authentic, and never to betray what is rightly called the "Augustinian charism" of a community life unified through love.

—Doctoral dissertation, 1987

## *Unity and Communion*

As can be seen from my episcopal motto, unity and communion are truly part of the charism of the Order of Saint Augustine, and also of my way of acting and thinking. I believe it is very important to promote communion in the Church, and we know well that communion, participation, and mission are the three key words of the Synod. So, as an Augustinian, for me promoting unity and communion is fundamental.

—Interview with Vatican News, 2023

## *The Augustinian Family*

We as Augustinians form a part of the Body of Christ, promoting unity in that spirituality of Saint Augustine and growing together as we search for the presence of God in our world and as we look for ways of sharing the Augustinian message, the spirituality of Saint

Augustine—that is, that particular way of looking at the Gospel—with one another and with the people around us. . . . Many of you are members of what we call secular fraternities—groups who are committed in a special way to the Augustinian Order and the life of the Order, and who have made even a certain kind of commitment in belonging to these various groups, and that are indeed part of the Augustinian family. Many other participants come from different kinds of groups of the Augustinian family—friends of Saint Augustine, those who gather together to reflect upon the Word of God or to commit yourselves in different kinds of service, outreach to people in need in the areas where you live and work. And you, too, find in the spirituality of Augustine something that is very meaningful in understanding the way to live the Gospel in today's world.

—Invitation for the Lay Augustinian Congress, 2012

## *One Body United in Christ*

The Body of Christ is such a wonderful image for us as Augustinians, as followers of Saint Augustine, and as brothers and sisters who together form truly one Body. We take on many forms. Some of those forms are friars and priests. Some of the forms are religious sisters of contemplative life and active life. Some of those forms are third order Augustinians and what we call today fraternities of secular Augustinians. Some of those forms are friends of Saint Augustine, followers of Saint Augustine, and other groups which also share with us the wonderful experience of living Augustinian spirituality. Each and every one of those is important, and we need each other, just as the eye needs the ear, as Saint Paul told us, and the foot needs the hand. All of us together form this one Body united in Christ. And I think it is so important that while we recognize the difference, we need to understand what it is that unites us, what brings us together. And obviously that's faith in Jesus Christ, and that's the wonderful experience that we have all had in some or another way of understanding how Saint Augustine and his spirituality has touched our lives. We have all been blessed by coming to know Augustine and by coming to know other Augustinians through Augustine, and for that we indeed give thanks.

—Address to the Lay Augustinian Congress, 2012

## *A Special Service to Offer*

Each and every one of us, in our own way, and with our specific gifts, has something to contribute to building up the whole Body of Christ. God has placed the members, each one of them, in the Body, just as he desired.

So it is that when we celebrate together as members of the Augustinian family, we are not all alike. We do not all have the same kind of service to give to the community. But together . . . each and every one of us—all of our groups, all of our communities included—do have a special service to offer in building up the Body of Christ, carrying out the mission of the Gospel.

—Homily for Mass for the Lay Augustinian Congress, 2012

## *The Gift of Friendship*

Different people can greatly enhance our lives. And, to

tell the truth, as an Augustinian, having a rich community built on the ability to share with others what happens to us, to be open to others, has been one of the greatest gifts I have been given in this life. The gift of friendship brings us back to Jesus himself.

—Interview with Ricardo Morales Jiménez, 2023

## *Nourished by the Word*

Since it is the Word of God which first brings people together into the Christian family (see canon 762), it is fitting and even necessary that a principal source of the unity in Augustinian life be found in a profound and frequent listening to the Word of God and to preaching which aids the members of the community to be strengthened in their vocation and in their apostolic work. Obviously it is not only the prior who can contribute in such a manner. Other members of the community as well as guest-homilists can certainly be encouraged to aid the community in an ever-deepening appreciation of the nourishment that is offered by the Scriptures.

—Doctoral dissertation, 1987

## *Specialists in Prayer*

Pope Paul VI spoke of religious as being called "specialists in prayer" (Discourse, October 28, 1966: AAS 58 (1966): 1155–1162). Today, too, there are many people who are searching for guidance in developing their own prayer life. Frequently they come looking for spiritual direction and help in developing this aspect of their faith. Thus, the importance of individual and common prayer on the part of Augustinians (and all religious) is paramount.

—Doctoral dissertation, 1987

## *The Liturgy of the Hours*

"Because of our particular relationship to the example of the early Christian community (see Acts 4:32; *Rule* chap. 1), Augustinians are called in a special way to common prayer. In this type of prayer we give expression to the very essence of the Church as community . . ." (*Constitutions* no. 95). The Liturgy of the Hours is the primary way in which the Order exercises this aspect of its prayer life. The Prayer of the Church, the way in which the Church responds to the exhortation of Christ to "pray without ceasing" (see Luke 18:1), is an expression of the unity of the entire Church.

—Doctoral dissertation, 1987

## *The Necessity of the Eucharist*

[The Eucharist's] fundamental place in the life of any community which calls itself Christian is well established. Just as Saint Augustine found the basis for his monastic ideal in the primitive community presented in the Acts of the Apostles, so too *Perfectae Caritatis* calls this model to mind in the importance of the Eucharist as part of the life of a religious community. The *Constitutions* likewise affirm the necessity of the Eucharist as the creative force of real Christian community (see *Constitutions* nn. 87–91).

—Doctoral dissertation, 1987

## *In Service of the Poor*

We as Augustinians, again as a mendicant order, I think are called to live a simple life at the service of others, and in a special way to reach out to those who are poor, the poor in society today, which includes of course those who are monetarily poor, but there are many other kinds of poverty in today's world. And Pope Francis is, I think, quite bold in challenging all of us in saying, "You, too, need to go out, to reach out, and to be close to others and to bring that message of Jesus Christ to them."

—Interview with Rome Reports, 2013

## *Augustinian Education*

The Order has for many, many years had a very important presence in the mission of education, of Catholic education, throughout Latin America. Of course, we have schools throughout the world today. . . . Augustinian education [is] a doorway that leads to the Gospel, announcing the kingdom of God. . . . Our role in education [is] indeed a very significant contribution to the role of the Church in education, to an understanding of how important it is to form young people today in those values that are fundamental to the Gospel, fundamental in our faith, fundamental to living a life that is dedicated to promoting values of justice and truth throughout the world.

—Invitation for the Congress of Augustinian Educators, 2012

5

# *On the Local Prior in the Order of Saint Augustine*

## *A Living Witness to the Order*

The local prior must be a living witness to the very nature of the Order, offering to the community inspiration to seek out a more radical adherence to those values which are fundamental to the Order. He must know the *Constitutions*, especially those numbers which deal with the nature and purpose of the Order (*Constitutions* nn. 7–17). Frequent reflection on the *Constitutions*, the *Rule*, and other sources of Augustinian spirituality would also be of great importance to him, as well as knowledge of the history of the Order and at least a general background in the thought of Saint Augustine.

—Doctoral dissertation, 1987

## *Knowledge, Experience, and Wisdom*

A superior must have a well-founded and well-integrated understanding of what is involved in being an Augustinian, and of what is expected of an authority within the Augustinian community. This only develops over a period of time lived in the Order, in which one can gradually gain the kind of knowledge, experience, and wisdom necessary. Thus, a three-year interval between the profession of solemn vows and the granting of eligibility for the office of local prior or local superior is a reasonable requirement.

—Doctoral dissertation, 1987

## *The Principle of Unity*

While Augustinian life places great emphasis on fraternity and collegiality—shown from a juridical point of view through the House Chapter—the prior's role as animator, leader, organizer, director, and teacher touches upon or is deeply integrated into the entire life of the community. For this reason, it would not be an exaggeration to speak of the local prior as the principle of unity for the local community. The *Constitutions* and the *Rule* speak frequently of the communion of the brothers, and while a great deal of responsibility for this experience of the common life rests upon each and every member of the community, it must be said that the prior has a particularly significant role in facilitating the sharing of life that is essential to Augustinian community. Whether it be in the area of the prayer life of the community, or in his efforts to create dialogue or bring about reconciliation, or in the celebration of birthdays or other significant events in the life of the brother, the prior is, as primus inter pares, the instrumental figure who can create, or deepen, the fraternal bond of communion among all the brothers. In a spirit of humility and service, and open to the help that he will need from all of the members of the community, the local prior will be able to fulfill those duties entrusted to him, and he will therefore aid the community in fulfilling its mission in the Church and in the world.

—Doctoral dissertation, 1987

## *Intent Upon God in Oneness of Mind and Heart*

In the first chapter of the *Rule*, Augustine wrote: "The main purpose for your having come together is to live harmoniously in your house, intent upon God in oneness of mind and heart" (*Rule* chap. 1). Life in the community is built upon the monastic ideal of Augustine, which he modeled upon the primitive Christian community in Jerusalem (Acts 4:32ff). "Saint Augustine . . . intended to renew the ideal of the sharing of goods that existed among the early Christians as a very suitable way to attain perfectly Christian love by living in a fraternal community in which we would all be 'intent upon God in oneness of mind and heart'" (*Constitutions* no. 66). Every dimension of the common life which strengthens unity among the brothers is an aid in fostering the search for God. "But we cannot seek God unless we have Christ, the Incarnate Word, as the way" (*Constitutions* no. 32). Every member of the community must play an active role in the realization of the communion of mind and heart in and through which the brothers seek God. The superior has the role of a kind of catalyst, but can do nothing if there is not an active cooperation on the part of each and every member of the community.

—Doctoral dissertation, 1987

## *A Leader of a Christian Community*

The prior's role ... must be considered as an ecclesial ministry. He is not merely an administrator within the community.... Augustinian community is modeled upon the monastic community of Saint Augustine, which in turn was based upon the ideal of the early Christian community as described in the Acts of the Apostles. Thus, the prior must be considered as a leader of a Christian community, with all that this concept entails. He is, for this very reason, empowered with the ministerial authority to teach, to sanctify, and to govern those who are entrusted to his care. Moreover, in as much as the consecrated life is recognized for the witness value it has within the Church, emphasizing in a particular way the mystery of salvation, the importance of the prior's ministry must not be underestimated.

—Doctoral dissertation, 1987

## *First Among Equals*

When speaking continually on the topic of the local superior, one might too easily forget or lose proper perspective of the value which must be found in the dimension of fraternal equality in the Augustinian Order. "Our Order is one of apostolic fraternity, that is a community of brothers who live with the People of God ..." (*Constitutions* no. 10). "Brotherhood in the Order, therefore, ought to be singularly evident in the equality of all the brothers, admitting of no privilege or honorary title" (*Constitutions* no. 12). It is within the context of the local community that the prior offers his service, and in terms of governance of the community, it is the prior as "first among equals" with the Chapter that best demonstrates this fraternity of the local level (*Constitutions* no. 13).

—Doctoral dissertation, 1987

## *In Charge as a Servant*

The idea that a superior's role is one of service is certainly not new. It is founded in the Gospel, and is also central to the Augustinian concept of authority. It is, nevertheless, a renewed emphasis on the fundamental purpose of authority that was all too frequently overlooked or ignored in the experience of far too many members of religious institutes. Instead of being a servant of others, the superior was a dominating ruler who was in many cases insensitive to those entrusted to his care. . . .

Elsewhere Augustine writes: "We are put in charge and we are servants; we possess authority, but only if we serve" [*Sermon* 340A.3]. There is no room in Augustine's concept of authority for one who is self-seeking and in search of power over others. The exercise of authority in any Christian community requires the setting aside of all self-interest and a total dedication to the good of the community. This is the attitude which must be adopted as the starting point for an authentic understanding of the role of the local superior.

—Doctoral dissertation, 1987

## *A Theology of Listening*

Theologically, an Augustinian community is an attempt to reconstitute the conditions of the first Christian community as described in the Acts of the Apostles and as adopted by Augustine in his *Rule*. In this community, authority is service, and that service is rendered within a context of listening to what the Spirit is saying in his people so that his projects can be carried out freely and willingly. The prior then is called to listen, so that together they can discern and implement what the Spirit inspires. This theology of listening as the Spirit welds the group into community provides a framework within which the Chapter's authority can be understood.

—Doctoral dissertation, 1987

## *Authority and Obedience*

Authority is an instrument, an aid which is provided for the sake of fulfilling the purpose of religious life. Its correlative, obedience, has, at least in the Augustinian context, much the same orientation. While obedience has a definite communal dimension (the word means "to listen to"), on the practical level it is rather contrived to think of obeying a team, a collegial authority. This is not, however, meant to lessen the importance of the involvement of the whole community in deciding certain issues, nor to underestimate the value of the Council in aiding a prior in the governance of the community.

—Doctoral dissertation, 1987

## *A Prudent Skipper*

Augustine's concept of authority and obedience in religious life was that they were to be means which, when necessary, would aid the community in its striving to live a life of perfect charity. Authority in the monastery is not an end in itself. The presence of a superior is to provide a service which renders the goal of religious life more readily attainable.

"The main purpose for your having come together is to live harmoniously in your house, intent upon God in oneness of mind and heart" (*Rule* chap. 1). Beginning his *Rule* of life in this way, Augustine clearly establishes that everything which in some way makes up or has a part in the living of the common life must be directed according to this precept. Writing in another place, Augustine expresses that the purpose of the governing authority in the monastery is to watch over the common life. Making the analogy of ships in a port, Augustine explains that those who choose to enter the religious life have in one sense a kind of freedom from many preoccupations. There are, however, dangers that a ship can encounter upon entering a port, and care must therefore be taken that these ships not collide into each other at the piers. "Let equality based on impartiality, and constant charity be observed. And when a strong wind enters the port from the open sea, a prudent skipper should intervene" (*Expositions of the Psalms* 99.10). Fraternal charity should be enough to maintain the peace and unity of the community. But when there are difficulties, there should be an authority which can prudently take action which will resolve the situation.

—Doctoral dissertation, 1987

## *Love the Person, Hate the Sin*

Let the prior keep in mind the important principle of

charity, remembering that the purpose of correcting one of the brothers is to seek his conversion and to safeguard the life of the community. Good judgment and sensitivity on the part of the prior will ensure that the best interests of all are sought, "all out of love for the person and hatred of sin" (*Rule* chap. 4).

—Doctoral dissertation, 1987

## *Retreats with Augustine*

Once a year each member of the Order is to make a retreat of at least five days (*Constitutions* no. 108). The retreat may be individual, or for the whole community, or organized in some other fashion. Such determination is not made in the *Constitutions*, and therefore it would depend upon the provincial, or the individual priors with their communities, to decide upon the way in which the annual retreat is to be made. It is recommended that these retreats include spiritual teaching of Saint Augustine, and also that the brothers renew their vows "so that the spirit of our following of Christ may be renewed and increased" (ibid.).

—Doctoral dissertation, 1987

## *Lay Fraternities*

Among the various groups which make up the entire Augustinian family, there are associations of laity who, while living a secular life, wish to follow more closely the Augustinian spirit of Christian living. . . . There are also societies of groups of the faithful, who, "imbued with the love of Saint Augustine and desirous of imitating him, have gathered together in Saint Augustine Societies without the duties and obligations of the other branches of the Order" (*Constitutions* no. 49).

Depending upon the statutes of these groups, and upon the way in which they are structured, it may frequently be the case that these groups are particularly associated to a specific local community of the Order. Especially in these cases, the local prior should seek to ensure that these groups receive the spiritual formation which is rightfully owed them by the Order. The Code places this responsibility upon the whole Order (canon 677, §2), but it is only logical that, unless other specific provisions are made, the local prior take it upon himself to see to it that these groups of the Augustinian family are given the opportunity to deepen the spirit of following Saint Augustine in their Christian lives.

—Doctoral dissertation, 1987

## *The Monk in Active Ministry*

Augustine wrote frequently about the difficulties of active ministry, about the "burden" involved in such work, and about the inevitable tension that exists for the monk who is called to active ministry due to the pressing needs of the Church. The very nature of the Order as it was founded in the thirteenth century includes active ministry, and there is thus a need to blend this aspect of service in the apostolate with the values of religious life that develop out of the more contemplative aspects of the Order. The local superior must be especially sensitive to such issues as it is he who is expected to offer guidance and leadership in such matters to the rest of the community.

—Doctoral dissertation, 1987

## *Examining One's Service*

Saint Augustine, in concluding the *Rule*, recommends that it be read weekly, serving as a mirror, so that no point in it might be neglected (*Rule* chap. 8). In much the same way, the superior would do well to consider frequently the counsels given in chapter seven of the *Rule* and in canons 618 and 619, so as to examine and evaluate his service to the community. In this way, he will be able to see where he has truly given what has been asked of him, and where he may still need to give more generously in his ministry of service to those who are entrusted to his care.

—Doctoral dissertation, 1987

# *Appendix A: Key Passages of Saint Augustine*

*Below are extracts from the writings of Saint Augustine with lines prominently quoted or referenced by Pope Leo XIV.*

## ***One in the One Christ***

All Christians, in union with their head who has ascended into heaven, form one Christ. It is not as though he were one and we many; no, we who are many are one in him, who is one [*in Illo uno unum*]. Christ, head and body together, is a single individual. What is his body? The Church, for the apostle tells us, "We are members of his body" (Eph. 5:30), and again, "You are Christ's body, and his members" (1 Cor. 12:27). Let us then listen to the voice of this single individual and understand it, for in his body we ourselves are this one man spoken of in the psalm, and in his body we shall see the good things of Jerusalem. . . .

The psalm hinted at this interpretation by expressing itself so obscurely that it warns us to knock at its door. It has covered its meaning in such a way that it invites us to shake it out. What I mean is this: It began with the plural: "Blessed are all who fear the Lord, and walk in his ways." It is obviously speaking here of many people but, because all these are one in Christ, it continues in the singular, promising, "You yourself shall eat the labors of your fruits." After saying in the plural, "Blessed are all who fear the Lord, and walk in his ways," why did it switch to the singular for its promise in the next verse?

Why "the labors of your fruits," rather than putting this in the plural? Did the psalmist forget so quickly that he was speaking to many people? Hardly. But, if you shake out his psalm, what will he tell you? "When I address many Christians, I understand them to be one in the one Christ," he will say. "You are many, and you are one single individual." We are many, and we are one individual. How can we be both many people and one individual? Because we cling inseparably to him of whom we are members; our head is in heaven, and he is drawing his members there after him.

—*Expositions of the Psalms*

## *For You a Bishop, With You a Christian*

From the moment this burden, about which such a difficult account has to be rendered, was placed on my shoulders, anxiety about the honor shown me has always indeed been haunting me. But this sort of consideration troubles me much more when the anniversary brings back afresh the old memory of that day, and sets it before my very eyes in such a way, that I feel as though I were coming up today to receive what I have already received all that time ago. What, though, is to be dreaded in this office, if not that I may take more pleasure, which is so dangerous, in the honor shown me, than in what bears fruit in your salvation? Let me therefore have the assistance of your prayers, that the one who did not disdain to bear with me may also deign to bear my burden with me. When you pray like that, you are also praying for yourselves. This burden of mine, you see, about which I am now speaking, what else is it, after all, but you? Pray for strength for me, just as I pray that you may not be too heavy.

I mean, the Lord Jesus wouldn't have called his burden light, if he wasn't going to carry it together with its porter. But you too must all support me, so that according to the apostle's instructions we may "carry one another's burdens, and in this way fulfill the law of Christ" (Gal. 6:2). If he doesn't carry it with us, we collapse; if he doesn't carry us, we keel over and die. Where I'm terrified by what I am for you, I am given comfort by what I am with you. For you I am a bishop, with you, after all, I am a Christian. The first is the name of an office undertaken, the second a name of grace; that one means danger, this one salvation. Finally, as if in the open sea, I am being tossed about by the stormy activity involved in that one; but as I recall by whose blood I have been redeemed, I enter a safe harbor in the tranquil recollection of this one; and thus while toiling away at my own proper office, I take my rest in the marvelous benefit conferred on all of us in common.

So I hope the fact that I have been bought together with you gives me more pleasure than my having been placed at your head; then, as the Lord has commanded, I will be more effectively your servant, and be preserved from ingratitude for the price by which I was bought to be, not too unworthily, your fellow servant.

—*Sermon* 340, "On the Anniversary of His Ordination"

## *Alexander the Great and the Pirate*

Remove justice, and what are kingdoms but gangs of criminals on a large scale? What are criminal gangs but petty kingdoms? A gang is a group of men under the command of a leader, bound by a compact of association, in which the plunder is divided according to an agreed convention.

If this villainy wins so many recruits from the ranks of the demoralized that it acquires territory, establishes a base, captures cities, and subdues peoples, it then openly arrogates to itself the title of kingdom, which is conferred on it in the eyes of the world, not by the renouncing of aggression but by the attainment of impunity.

For it was a witty and a truthful rejoinder which was given by a captured pirate to Alexander the Great. The king asked the fellow, "What is your idea, in infesting the sea?" And the pirate answered, with uninhibited insolence, "The same as yours, in infesting the earth! But because I do it with a tiny craft, I'm called a pirate: Because you have a mighty navy, you're called an emperor."

—*City of God*

## *The Restless Heart*

Great art Thou, "O Lord, and greatly to be praised; great is Thy power" (Ps. 96:4; cf. 145:3), and "of Thy wisdom there is no number" (Ps. 147:5). And man desires to praise Thee. He is but a tiny part of all that Thou hast created. He bears about him his mortality, the evidence of his sinfulness, and the evidence that "Thou dost resist the proud" (Prov. 3:34; 1 Pet. 5:5; Jas. 4:6): Yet this tiny part of all that Thou hast created desires to praise Thee.

Thou dost so excite him that to praise Thee is his joy. For Thou hast made us for Thyself and our hearts are restless till they rest in Thee. Grant me, O Lord, to know which is the soul's first movement toward Thee—to implore Thy aid or to utter its praise of Thee; and whether it must know Thee before it can implore. For it would seem clear that no one can call upon Thee without knowing Thee, for if he did he might invoke another than Thee, knowing Thee not. Yet may it be that a man must implore Thee before he can know Thee? But, "how shall they call on Him in whom they have not believed? or how shall they believe without a preacher?" (Rom. 10:13–14). And, "they shall praise the Lord that seek Him" (Ps. 22:26); for those that seek shall find (see Matt. 7:7–8; Luke 11:9–10); and finding Him they will praise Him. Let me seek Thee, Lord, by praying Thy aid, and let me utter my prayer believing in Thee: For Thou hast been preached to us. My faith, Lord, cries to Thee, the faith that Thou hast given me, that Thou hast inbreathed in me, through the humanity of Thy Son and by the ministry of Thy preacher.

—*Confessions*

# *Appendix B: "The Rule of Saint Augustine"*

*Below is "The Rule of Saint Augustine," written around the year 400—the oldest monastic rule in the history of the Western Church. It is still observed by thousands of men and women religious around the world.*

## Chapter I
## Purpose and Basis of Common Life

Before all else, dear brothers, love God and then your neighbor, because these are the chief commandments given to us.

1. The following are the precepts we order you living in the monastery to observe.

2. The main purpose for you having come together is to live harmoniously in your house, intent upon God in oneness of mind and heart.

3. Call nothing your own, but let everything be yours in common. Food and clothing shall be distributed to each of you by your superior, not equally to all, for all do not enjoy equal health, but rather according to each one's need. For so you read in the Acts of the Apostles that "they had all things in common and distribution was made to each one according to each one's need" (4:32, 35).

4. Those who owned something in the world should be

careful in wanting to share it in common once they have entered the monastery.

5. But they who owned nothing should not look for those things in the monastery that they were unable to have in the world. Nevertheless, they are to be given all that their health requires even if, during their time in the world, poverty made it impossible for them to find the very necessities of life. And those should not consider themselves fortunate because they have found the kind of food and clothing which they were unable to find in the world.

6. And let them not hold their heads high, because they associate with people whom they did not dare to approach in the world, but let them rather lift up their hearts and not seek after what is vain and earthly. Otherwise, monasteries will come to serve a useful purpose for the rich and not the poor, if the rich are made humble there and the poor are puffed up with pride.

7. The rich, for their part, who seemed important in the world, must not look down upon their brothers who have come into this holy brotherhood from a condition of poverty. They should seek to glory in the fellowship of poor brothers rather than in the reputation of rich relatives. They should neither be elated if they have contributed a part of their wealth to the common life, nor take more pride in sharing their riches with the monastery than if they were to enjoy them in the world. Indeed, every other kind of sin has to do with the commission of evil deeds, whereas pride lurks even in good works

in order to destroy them. And what good is it to scatter one's wealth abroad by giving to the poor, even to become poor oneself, when the unhappy soul is thereby more given to pride in despising riches than it had been in possessing them?

8. Let all of you then live together in oneness of mind and heart, mutually honoring God in yourselves, whose temples you have become.

---

## Chapter II
## Prayer

1. "Be assiduous in prayer" (Col. 4:2), at the hours and times appointed.

2. In the Oratory no one should do anything other than that for which it was intended and from which it also takes its name. Consequently, if there are some who might wish to pray there during their free time, even outside the hours appointed, they should not be hindered by those who think something else must be done there.

3. When you pray to God in Psalms and hymns, think over in your hearts the words that come from your lips.

4. Chant only what is prescribed for chant; moreover, let nothing be chanted unless it is so prescribed.

---

## Chapter III
## Moderation and Self-Denial

1. Subdue the flesh, so far as your health permits, by fasting and abstinence from food and drink. However, when someone is unable to fast, he should still take no food outside mealtimes unless he is ill.

2. When you come to table, listen until you leave to what is the custom to read, without disturbance or strife. Let not your mouths alone take nourishment but let your hearts too hunger for the words of God.

3. If those in more delicate health from their former way of life are treated differently in the matter of food, this should not be a source of annoyance to the others or appear unjust in the eyes of those who owe their stronger health to different habits of life. Nor should the healthier brothers deem them more fortunate for having food which they do not have, but rather consider themselves fortunate for having the good health which the others do not enjoy.

4. And if something in the way of food, clothing, and bedding is given to those coming to the monastery from a more genteel way of life, which is not given to those who are stronger, and therefore happier, then these latter ought to consider how far these others have come in passing from their life in the world down to this life of ours, though they have been unable to reach the level of frugality common to the stronger brothers. Nor should all want to receive what they see given in larger measure

to the few, not as a token of honor, but as a help to support them in their weakness. This would give rise to a deplorable disorder—that in the monastery, where the rich are coming to bear as much hardship as they can, the poor are turning to a more genteel way of life.

5. And just as the sick must take less food to avoid discomfort, so too, after their illness, they are to receive the kind of treatment that will quickly restore their strength, even though they come from a life of extreme poverty. Their more recent illness has, as it were, afforded them what accrued to the rich as part of their former way of life. But when they have recovered their former strength, they should go back to their happier way of life which, because their needs are fewer, is all the more in keeping with God's servants. Once in good health, they must not become slaves to the enjoyment of food which was necessary to sustain them in their illness. For it is better to suffer a little want than to have too much.

## Chapter IV
## Safeguarding Chastity, and Fraternal Correction

1. There should be nothing about your clothing to attract attention. Besides, you should not seek to please by your apparel, but by a good life.

2. Whenever you go out, walk together, and when you reach your destination, stay together.

3. In your walk, deportment, and in all actions, let nothing occur to give offense to anyone who sees you, but only what becomes your holy state of life.

4. Although your eyes may chance to rest upon some woman or other, you must not fix your gaze upon any woman. Seeing women when you go out is not forbidden, but it is sinful to desire them or to wish them to desire you, for it is not by tough or passionate feeling alone but by one's gaze also that lustful desires mutually arise. And do not say that your hearts are pure if there is immodesty of the eye, because the unchaste eye carries the message of an impure heart. And when such hearts disclose their unchaste desires in a mutual gaze, even without saying a word, then it is that chastity suddenly goes out of their life, even though their bodies remain unsullied by unchaste acts.

5. And whoever fixes his gaze upon a woman and likes to have hers fixed upon him must not suppose that others do not see what he is doing. He is very much seen, even by those he thinks do not see him. But suppose all this escapes the notice of man—what will he do about God who sees from on high and from whom nothing is hidden? Or are we to imagine that he does not see because he sees with a patience as great as his wisdom? Let the religious man then have such fear of God that he will not want to be an occasion of sinful pleasure to a woman. Ever mindful that God sees all things, let him not desire to look at a woman lustfully. For it is on this point that fear of the Lord is recommended, where it is written:

"An abomination to the Lord is he who fixes his gaze" (Prov. 27:20).

6. So when you are together in church and anywhere else where women are present, exercise a mutual care over purity of life. Thus, by mutual vigilance over one another will God, who dwells in you, grant you his protection.

7. If you notice in someone of your brothers this wantonness of the eye, of which I am speaking, admonish him at once so that the beginning of evil will not grow more serious but will be promptly corrected.

8. But if you see him doing the same thing again on some other day, even after your admonition, then whoever had occasion to discover this must report him as he would a wounded man in need of treatment. But let the offense first be pointed out to two or three so that he can be proven guilty on the testimony of these two or three and be punished with due severity. And do not charge yourselves with ill-will when you bring this offense to light. Indeed, yours is the greater blame if you allow your brothers to be lost through your silence when you are able to bring about their correction by your disclosure. If your brother, for example, were suffering a bodily wound that he wanted to hide for fear of undergoing treatment, would it not be cruel of you to remain silent and a mercy on your part to make this known? How much greater then is your obligation to make his condition known lest he continue to suffer a more deadly wound of the soul.

9. But if he fails to correct the fault despite this admonition, he should first be brought to the attention of the superior before the offense is made known to the others who will have to prove his guilt, in the event he denies the charge. Thus, corrected in private, his fault can perhaps be kept from the others. But should he feign ignorance, the others are to be summoned so that in the presence of all he can be proven guilty, rather than stand accused on the word of one alone. Once proven guilty, he must undergo salutary punishment according to the judgment of the superior or priest having the proper authority. If he refuses to submit to punishment, he shall be expelled from your brotherhood even if he does not withdraw of his own accord. For this too is not done out of cruelty, but from a sense of compassion so that many others may not be lost through his bad example.

10. And let everything I have said about not fixing one's gaze be also observed carefully and faithfully with regard to other offenses: to find them out, to ward them off, to make them known, to prove and punish them—all out of love for man and a hatred of sin.

11. But if anyone should go so far in wrongdoing as to receive letters in secret from any woman, or small gifts of any kind, you ought to show mercy and pray for him if he confesses this of his own accord. But if the offense is detected and he is found guilty, he must be more severely chastised according to the judgment of the priest or superior.

---

## Chapter V
## The Care of Community Goods and Treatment of the Sick

1. Keep your clothing in one place in charge of one or two, or of as many as are needed to care for them and to prevent damage from moths. And just as you have your food from the one pantry, so, too, you are to receive your clothing from a single wardrobe. If possible, do not be concerned about what you are given to wear at the change of seasons, whether each of you gets back what he had put away or something different, providing no one is denied what he needs. If, however, disputes and murmuring arise on this account because someone complains that he received poorer clothing than he had before, and thinks it is beneath him to wear the kind of clothing worn by another, you may judge from this how lacking you are in that holy and inner garment of the heart when you quarrel over garments for the body. But if allowance is made for your weakness and you do receive the same clothing you had put away, you must still keep it in one place under the common charge.

2. In this way, no one shall perform any task for his own benefit but all your work shall be done for the common good, with greater zeal and more dispatch than if each one of you were to work for yourself alone. For charity, as it is written, "is not self-seeking" (1 Cor. 13:5), meaning that it places the common good before its own, not its own before the common good. So whenever you show greater concern for the common good than for your own, you may know that you are growing in charity. Thus, let

the abiding virtue of charity prevail in all things that minister to the fleeting necessities of life.

3. It follows, therefore, that if anyone brings something for their sons or other relatives living in the monastery, whether a garment or anything else they think is needed, this must not be accepted secretly as one's own but must be placed at the disposal of the superior so that, as common property, it can be given to whoever needs it. But if someone secretly keeps something given to him, he shall be judged guilty of theft.

4. Your clothing should be cleaned either by yourselves or by those who perform this service, as the superior shall determine, so that too great a desire for clean clothing may not be the source of interior stains on the soul.

5. As for bodily cleanliness too, a brother must never deny himself the use of the bath when his health requires it. But this should be done on medical advice, without complaining, so that even though unwilling, he shall do what has to be done for his health when the superior orders it. However, if the brother wishes it, when it might not be good for him, you must not comply with his desire, for sometimes we think something is beneficial for the pleasure it gives, even though it may prove harmful.

6. Finally, if the cause of a brother's bodily pain is not apparent, you must take the word of God's servant when he indicates what is giving him pain. But if it remains uncertain whether the remedy he likes is good for him, a doctor should be consulted.

7. When there is need to frequent the public baths or any other place, no fewer than two or three should go together, and whoever has to go somewhere must not go with those of his own choice but with those designated by the superior.

8. The care of the sick, whether those in convalescence or others suffering from some indisposition, even though free of fever, shall be assigned to a brother who can personally obtain from the pantry whatever he sees is necessary for each one.

9. Those in charge of the pantry, or of clothing and books, should render cheerful service to their brothers.

10. Books are to be requested at a fixed hour each day, and anyone coming outside that hour is not to receive them.

11. But as for clothing and shoes, those in charge shall not delay the giving of them whenever they are required by those in need of them.

---

## Chapter VI
## Asking Pardon and Forgiving Offenses

1. You should either avoid quarrels altogether or else put an end to them as quickly as possible; otherwise, anger may grow into hatred, making a plank out of a splinter, and turn the soul into a murderer. For so you read: "Everyone who hates his brother is a murderer" (1 John 3:15).

2. Whoever has injured another by open insult, or by abusive or even incriminating language, must remember to repair the injury as quickly as possible by an apology, and he who suffered the injury must also forgive, without further wrangling. But if they have offended one another, they must forgive one another's trespasses for the sake of your prayers, which should be recited with greater sincerity each time you repeat them. Although a brother is often tempted to anger, yet prompt to ask pardon from one he admits to having offended, such a one is better than another who, though less given to anger, finds it too hard to ask forgiveness. But a brother who is never willing to ask pardon, or does not do so from his heart, has no reason to be in the monastery, even if he is not expelled. You must then avoid being too harsh in your words, and should they escape your lips, let those same lips not be ashamed to heal the wounds they have caused.

3. But whenever the good of discipline requires you to speak harshly in correcting your subjects, then, even if you think you have been unduly harsh in your language, you are not required to ask forgiveness lest, by practicing too great humility toward those who should be your subjects, the authority to rule is undermined. But you should still ask forgiveness from the Lord of all who knows with what deep affection you love even those whom you might happen to correct with undue severity. Besides, you are to love another with a spiritual rather than an earthly love.

---

## Chapter VII
## Governance and Obedience

1. The superior should be obeyed as a father with the respect due him so as not to offend God in his person, and, even more so, the priest who bears responsibility for you all.

2. But it shall pertain chiefly to the superior to see that these precepts are all observed and, if any point has been neglected, to take care that the transgression is not carelessly overlooked but is punished and corrected. In doing so, he must refer whatever exceeds the limit and power of his office, to the priest who enjoys greater authority among you.

3. The superior, for his part, must not think himself fortunate in his exercise of authority but in his role as one serving you in love. In your eyes he shall hold the first place among you by the dignity of his office, but in fear before God he shall be as the least among you. He must show himself as an example of good works toward all. "Let him admonish the unruly, cheer the fainthearted, support the weak, and be patient toward all" (1 Thess. 5:14). Let him uphold discipline while instilling fear. And though both are necessary, he should strive to be loved by you rather than feared, ever mindful that he must give an account of you to God.

4. It is by being more obedient, therefore, that you show mercy not only toward yourselves but also toward the

superior whose higher rank among you exposes him all the more to greater peril.

---

## Chapter VIII
## Observance of the Rule

1. The Lord grant that you may observe all these precepts in a spirit of charity as lovers of spiritual beauty, giving forth the good odor of Christ in the holiness of your lives: not as slaves living under the law but as men living in freedom under grace.

2. And that you may see yourselves in this little book, as in a mirror, have it read to you once a week so as to neglect no point through forgetfulness. When you find that you are doing all that has been written, give thanks to the Lord, the Giver of every good. But when one of you finds that he has failed on any point, let him be sorry for the past, be on his guard for the future, praying that he will be forgiven his fault and not be led into temptation.

# Notes

*Minor style adjustments have occasionally been made on excerpted material for consistency and readability. All references to the "Expositions of the Psalms" follow the Vulgate numbering used by Saint Augustine rather than the Masoretic numbering used in most modern translations.*

**vi Epigraph:** Leo XIV, "First Blessing *Urbi et Orbi*," May 8, 2025, vatican.va.

## 1. On Saint Augustine's Life and Works

**1 Beginning with Biography:** Robert F. Prevost, foreword to *Saint Augustine* (Mercatorfonds, 2007), 7.

**2 The Grace and Peace of God:** Leo XIV, "Video Message to the Augustinian Province of Saint Thomas of Villanova," August 29, 2025, vatican.va.

**2 A Summary of Augustine's Ministry:** "San Agustín - Obispo - Mons. Robert Prevost Martínez OSA," Parroquia N. S. del Rosario – Chitré, August 25, 2020, YouTube, 4:10–13:08, trans. María Leyva Zapata, https://youtu.be/f_oWOFnbCZw.

**6 Preferential Love for the Poor:** Leo XIV, *Dilexi Te*, apostolic exhortation, October 4, 2025, vatican.va.

**6 Monk-Bishops:** Robert F. Prevost, *The Office and Authority of the Local Prior in the Order of Saint Augustine* (The Catholic University of America Press, 2025), 42n18.

**7 Opening a Window:** "Augustinians to meet in Rome to choose new leader and discuss future plans," ROME REPORTS in English, August 27, 2013, YouTube, 0:54–1:15, https://youtu.be/qd6IjYQStFo.

**7 The *Confessions* and Human Experience:** "Pope Leo on

media and evangelization. Full 2012 interview," Catholic News Service, posted May 10, 2025, YouTube, 28:05–31:48, https://youtu.be/QXVkJ5TQi1s.

9 ***The City of God* Today:** Leo XIV, "Address to Participants in the Sixteenth Annual Meeting of the International Catholic Legislators Network," August 23, 2025, vatican.va.

10 **A Response to the Secular World:** "Pope Leo XIV on the counterculture of the new evangelization (Part 2 of 2)," Catholic News Service, November 9, 2012, YouTube, https://youtu.be/uLkGBuoy1pQ.

11 **The Myths of Secular Society:** "Pope Leo on media and evangelization," YouTube, 4:17–5:40, https://youtu.be/QXVkJ5TQi1s.

11 ***De Magistro* and the Inner Master:** Leo XIV, "Greeting to the Augustinian Sisters, Servants of Jesus and Mary," July 5, 2025, vatican.va.

12 **The First Modern Man:** Prevost, foreword to *Saint Augustine*, 7.

## 2. On Saint Augustine's Spirituality

13 **Made Restless by History:** Leo XIV, homily, Mass for the Beginning of the Pontificate, May 18, 2025, vatican.va.

13 **Begin with Your Own Heart:** Leo XIV, "Video Message to the Young People of Chicago and the Whole World," June 14, 2025, vatican.va.

14 **Return to the Heart:** Leo XIV, meditation, Jubilee of Seminarians, June 24, 2025, vatican.va.

14 **God Is Closer to Us than We Are to Ourselves:** "Pope Leo on media and evangelization. Full 2012 interview," Catholic

News Service, posted May 10, 2025, YouTube, 1:11–2:03, https://youtu.be/QXVkJ5TQi1s.

**15 The Secret of Hope:** Leo XIV, "Message for the 9th World Day of the Poor," June 13, 2025, vatican.va.

**15 I Burned for Your Peace:** Leo XIV, homily, Mass for the Jubilee of Youth at Tor Vergata, August 3, 2025, vatican.va.

**16 God Is Your Everything:** Leo XIV, "Address to the Representatives of Certain Women's Religious Institutes," June 30, 2025, vatican.va.

**17 Lord, Your Works Praise You:** Leo XIV, homily, Mass for the Care of Creation, July 9, 2025, vatican.va.

**17 Do Not Delay!:** Leo XIV, general audience, June 4, 2025, vatican.va.

**18 Living Up to Our Calling:** Leo XIV, general audience, June 11, 2025, vatican.va.

**19 The Man Who Was Needed:** Leo XIV, general audience, June 18, 2025, vatican.va.

**20 Faith Touches:** Leo XIV, general audience, June 25, 2025, vatican.va.

**20 Grant What You Command, Command What You Will:** Leo XIV, "Message of the Holy Father Leo XIV to the Participants in the Commemoration of 500 Years of the Anabaptist Movement," May 29, 2025, vatican.va.

**21 The Holy Spirit Descends Upon Us:** Leo XIV, homily, Solemnity of Pentecost, Jubilee of Movements, Associations, and New Communities, June 8, 2025, vatican.va.

**21 Both Listening and Service:** Leo XIV, homily, Mass at the Cathedral of Albano, July 20, 2025, vatican.va.

22 **Let Us Forgive:** Leo XIV, "Address to Participants in the General Chapters of the Society of African Missions, of the Third Order Regular of Saint Francis, of the Formators of the Servants of the Paraclete," June 6, 2025, vatican.va.

22 **Becoming the Good Samaritan:** Leo XIV, homily, Mass at the Pontifical Parish of Saint Thomas of Villanova (Castel Gandolfo), July 13, 2025, vatican.va.

23 **Transformation in Love:** Leo XIV, angelus, August 10, 2025, vatican.va.

23 **Following Christ Means Joining the Church:** "Interview with Cardinal Robert Prevost OSA: 'Above all, a bishop must proclaim Jesus Christ,'" Order of Saint Augustine, updated May 8, 2025, https://www.augustinianorder.org/post/interview-with-cardinal-robert-prevost-osa-above-all-a-bishop-must-proclaim-jesus-christ.

24 **No One Is Christian Alone:** Leo XIV, "Address to the Moderators of Lay Associations, Ecclesial Movements, and New Communities," June 6, 2025, vatican.va.

25 **Bread That Restores and Does Not Run Short:** Leo XIV, homily, Solemnity of the Most Holy Body and Blood of Christ, June 22, 2025, vatican.va.

25 **The Sacrifice and Gift of Love:** Leo XIV, angelus, Most Holy Body and Blood of Christ, June 22, 2025, vatican.va.

26 **Harmony in Diversity:** Leo XIV, homily, Mass and blessing of the sacred pallium for the new metropolitan archbishops on the Solemnity of Saints Peter and Paul, June 29, 2025, vatican.va.

26 **A Family of God:** Leo XIV, "Address of the Holy Father to Pontifical Missions Societies," May 22, 2025, vatican.va.

**27 A Sign of Unity:** Leo XIV, homily for the Mass for the Beginning of the Pontificate, vatican.va.

**28 We Will All Be One:** Leo XIV, homily, Mass for the Jubilee of Families, Children, Grandparents, and the Elderly, June 1, 2025, vatican.va.

**28 The Communion of Christians:** Leo XIV, homily, Mass and priestly ordinations for the Jubilee of Priests, June 27, 2025, vatican.va.

**28 Listening as Much as Possible:** Leo XIV, homily, Mass for the possession of the chair of the bishop of Rome, May 25, 2025, vatican.va.

**29 The Mindset of Synodality:** Leo XIV, "Address to the Italian Episcopal Conference," June 17, 2025, vatican.va.

**29 The *Amoris Officium*:** Leo XIV, meditation, Jubilee of Bishops, June 25, 2025, vatican.va.

**30 One Flock and One Shepherd:** Leo XIV, "Address to the Clergy of the Diocese of Rome," June 12, 2025, vatican.va.

## 3. On Saint Augustine's Thought

**31 Eschatology, Anthropology, and Christian Hope:** Robert F. Prevost, foreword to *Augustine on the Hope of Groaning Creation* by Mamerto A. Alfeche (University of San Agustin Publishing House, 2006), v–vii.

**34 Why Do You Stand in Your Own Strength?:** Leo XIV, address to the seminarians of the dioceses of Triveneto, June 25, 2025, vatican.va.

**35 Chosen Before Choosing:** Leo XIV, homily, visit to the Tomb of Saint Paul, May 20, 2025, vatican.va.

**35 Thirst for the Infinite:** Leo XIV, "Message to Participants in the Seminar 'Evangelizing with the Families of Today and Tomorrow: Ecclesiological and Pastoral Challenges,' Organized by the Dicastery for Laity, Family, and Life," May 28, 2025, vatican.va.

36 **The Trinity and Divine Wisdom:** Leo XIV, homily, Solemnity of the Holy Trinity, Jubilee of Sport, June 15, 2025, vatican.va.

37 **Devouring the Word:** "The Papacy of Reason — Inside the Mind of Benedict XVI," Edward Pentin, posted January 9, 2023, YouTube, 8:28–9:03, https://youtu.be/SAqN3jSlKd8.

37 **Seeds Sown in the Universe:** Leo XIV, "Address to the Participants of the Summer School of Astrophysics Promoted by the Vatican Observatory," June 16, 2025, vatican.va.

38 **Building the City of God:** Leo XIV, "Address to Members of the International Inter-Parliamentary Union," June 21, 2025, vatican.va.

38 **We Are the Times:** Leo XIV, "Address to Representatives of the Media," May 12, 2025, vatican.va.

39 **Augustine's Theory of Education:** Robert F. Prevost, *The Office and Authority of the Local Prior in the Order of Saint Augustine* (The Catholic University of America Press, 2025), 89n1.

39 **Let Us Sing:** "Address to Participants in the Event Promoted by the Cardinal Domenico Bartolucci Foundation," June 18, 2025, vatican.va.

40 **Augustine on Friendship:** Leo XIV, "Dialogue Between His Holiness Pope Leo XIV and Young People During the Jubilee Vigil," August 2, 2025, vatican.va.

40 **Augustine on Old Age:** Leo XIV, "Message for the Fifth

World Day for Grandparents and the Elderly 2025," July 27, 2025, vatican.va.

41 **Augustine on Mourning:** Leo XIV, "Words of the Holy Father Leo XIV to Young Egyptian Pilgrims, Who Have Come to Rome for the Jubilee of Youth with the Young Pascale Rafic," August 2, 2025, vatican.va.

41 **A Great Debt:** "Evening of Reflection with Cardinal Prevost and Mass," LIVEMass StJude, August 7, 2024, YouTube, 12:07–12:37, https://youtu.be/9U3yBFdt4QM.

## 4. On the Order of Saint Augustine

43 **Two Great Sources:** Robert F. Prevost, *The Office and Authority of the Local Prior in the Order of Saint Augustine* (The Catholic University of America Press, 2025), 92–93.

44 **Unity and Communion:** Leo XIV, 2023 interview with Vatican News, cited in "Pope Leo XIV's motto and coat of arms," May 10, 2025, https://www.vaticannews.va/en/pope/news/2025-05/pope-leo-xiv-s-motto-and-coat-of-arms.html.

44 **The Augustinian Family:** "III Lay Augustinian Congress," CuriaGenAgostiniana, June 13, 2012, YouTube, 0:55–1:20, 1:29–2:22, https://youtu.be/X9jYXaIOeK8.

45 **One Body United in Christ:** "III Lay Augustinian Congress - Speech of Father Robert F. Prevost," CuriaGenAgostiniana, July 19, 2012, YouTube, 1:01–2:43, https://youtu.be/Q_k3t2ZqRPs.

46 **A Special Service to Offer:** "III Lay Augustinian Congress - Homily of prior General," CuriaGenAgostiniana, July 15, 2012, YouTube, 4:29–5:14, https://youtu.be/lWyRax4ZiZQ.

46 **The Gift of Friendship:** "Interview with Cardinal Robert

Prevost OSA: 'Above all, a bishop must proclaim Jesus Christ,'" Order of Saint Augustine, updated May 8, 2025, https://www.augustinianorder.org/post/interview-with-cardinal-robert-prevost-osa-above-all-a-bishop-must-proclaim-jesus-christ.

47 **Nourished by the Word:** Prevost, *The Office and Authority of the Local Prior in the Order of Saint Augustine*, 105.

47 **Specialists in Prayer:** Prevost, 118.

48 **The Liturgy of the Hours:** Prevost, 119.

48 **The Necessity of the Eucharist:** Prevost, 126.

49 **In Service of the Poor:** "Augustinians to meet in Rome to choose new leader and discuss future plans," ROME REPORTS in English, August 27, 2013, YouTube, 1:22–1:53, https://youtu.be/qd6IjYQStFo.

49 **Augustinian Education:** "Congress of Augustinian Educators & Schools - Message of Robert Prevost OSA," Curia-GenAgostiniana, June 19, 2012, YouTube, 0:32–0:44, 0:59–1:07, 1:12–1:39, https://youtu.be/1SMM5_lQcKo.

## 5. On the Local Prior in the Order of Saint Augustine

50 **A Living Witness to the Order:** Robert F. Prevost, *The Office and Authority of the Local Prior in the Order of Saint Augustine* (The Catholic University of America Press, 2025), 92.

50 **Knowledge, Experience, and Wisdom:** Prevost, 76.

51 **The Principle of Unity:** Prevost, 190–91.

52 **Intent Upon God in Oneness of Mind and Heart:** Prevost, 24–25.

53 **A Leader of a Christian Community:** Prevost, 189–90.

**53 First Among Equals:** Prevost, 155–56.

**54 In Charge as a Servant:** Prevost, 15–16.

**54 A Theology of Listening:** Prevost, 159–60.

**55 Authority and Obedience:** Prevost, 58–59.

**55 A Prudent Skipper:** Prevost, 12–13.

**56 Love the Person, Hate the Sin:** Prevost, 185.

**57 Retreats with Augustine:** Prevost, 124–25.

**57 Lay Fraternities:** Prevost, 110–11.

**58 The Monk in Active Ministry:** Prevost, 23–24.

**59 Examining One's Service:** Prevost, 33.

## Appendix A: Key Passages of Saint Augustine

**60 One in the One Christ:** Augustine, exposition of Psalm 127.3–4, in *The Works of Saint Augustine: A Translation for the 21st Century, Expositions of the Psalms III/20 (121–150)*, trans. Maria Boulding, ed. Boniface Ramsey (New City, 2004), 101.

**61 For You a Bishop, With You a Christian:** Augustine, *Sermon* 340.1, "On the Anniversary of His Ordination," in *The Works of Saint Augustine: A Translation for the 21st Century, Sermons III/9 (306–340A): On the Saints*, trans. Edmund Hill (New City, 1994), 292–93.

**62 Alexander the Great and the Pirate:** Augustine, *City of God* 4.4, trans. Henry Bettenson (Penguin, 2003), 139.

**63 The Restless Heart:** Augustine, *Confessions* 1.1, trans. F. J. Sheed (Word on Fire Classics, 2017), 2. The reference to "Thy preacher" is likely to Saint Ambrose, bishop of Milan (339–397). Cf. Augustine, *Letter* 147.52.

## Appendix B: *The Rule of Saint Augustine*

This translation by Robert Russell, OSA, is based on the critical text of Luc Verheijen, OSA (*La regle de saint Augustin*, Etudes Augustiniennes, Paris, 1967). Two sentences not contained in the critical text have been included to conform with the official text published with the *Constitutiones Ordinis Fratrum S. Augustini* (Rome, 1968). They are the opening sentence of the *Rule* and the following one from Chapter VI: "But if someone secretly keeps something given to him, he shall be judged guilty of theft."